THIS NOTEBOOK BELONGS TO

NAME _____

SURNAME _____

ELDER FUTHARK

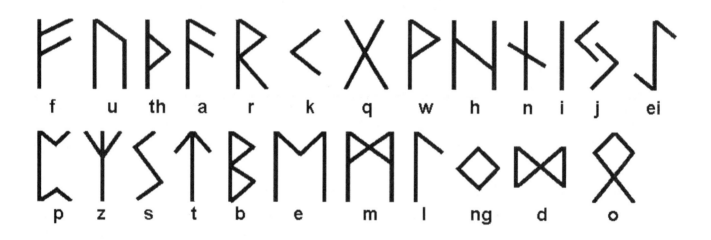

f u th a r k q w h n i j ei

p z s t b e m l ng d o

THE ELDER FUTHARK, USED FOR WRITING PROTO-NORSE, CONSISTS OF 24 RUNES THAT OFTEN ARE ARRANGED IN THREE GROUPS OF EIGHT; EACH GROUP IS REFERRED TO AS AN ÆTT (OLD NORSE, MEANING 'CLAN, GROUP').

Name: Ansuz, "an Aesir god."
Phoneme: A (long and/or short).
Meaning: prosperity, vitality.

ANSUZ

Stands for:	God, Ancestral God
Sound	"A"
Gods	Odin, Loki
Colour	Purple
Element	Air
Astrology	Pluto, Mercury
Energy	Masculine
Health	Mouth, Throat, Thyroid
Key Words	Order, Transformation, Knowledge, Inspiration

RUNE ANSUZ ELDER FUTHARK MEANING.

"Find your ears before you search for words."

Ansuz – "Anne – suhz" – Literally: "Woden" – Esoteric: "Breath" or "Ancestral Sovereign God"

Key Concepts: order, gods, Odin, transmission of intelligence, communication, reason, inspiration, language, breath, sound, origins of language, the Voice of the Universe, spellsong, casting, chanting, ancestors, passing of the breath along the ancestral line, evolution of gods, speech, poetry, discussion of runes, memetics, semiotics, etymology, linguistics.

Psi: mental stability, communion, inspiration, listening

Energy: sovereign ancestral god, animating spirit, breath, communication, exploration, order, answers

Mundane: words, conversation, symbols, elders, music

Divinations: Divine inspiration, word-power, synthesis, transformation, intellect, open paths of communication; or misunderstanding, delusion, manipulation by others, boredom, bad advice

Governs:
All powers of naming and conceptualization
Convincing and magnetic speech and writing, and the power of suggestion and hypnosis
Acquisition of creative wisdom, inspiration, ecstasy and divine communication
Reason, analysis and good advice
Connecting and networking
Listening to oneself and one's own particular inner-voice

Ansuz is the rune representing wisdom, knowledge, and communication. All in all, it is the rune of the transmission and reception of information. Information that is understandable and usable.

Ansuz is complex rune, and its energies and manifestations are very predominant in our time. The common interpretation is that this rune signifies "a god", that is, one of the Aesir, particularly Odin. It refers to a personal ancestry that traces back to the old gods, and therefor our divine inheritance. It is also linked to the mouth, breath and speech, persuasion and inspiration.

B

Name: Berkanan, "birch."
Phoneme: B.
Meaning: fertility, growth, sustenance.

BERKANAN OR BERKANO

Stands for:	Birch Goddess
Sound	"B"
Gods	Berchta, Holda, Frigg
Colour	Green
Element	Earth
Astrology	Virgo
Energy	Female
Health	Reproductive Health
Key Words	Fertility, Abundance, Birch Tree, Ancestry, Gestation

RUNE BERKANO ELDER FUTHARK MEANING.

"The most obvious Truth is hidden deep within, and only you will ever know it."

Berkano – "Burr-can-oh" – Literally: "Birch Goddess" – Esoteric: Birth, Sanctuary

Rune of continued growth and continual rebirth or renewal in all things. The rune of becoming.

Psi: secrecy, silence, safety, mature wisdom, dependence

Energy: container/releaser, female fertility, trees and plantlife

Mundane: motherhood, healing, gardening, child raising, the womb

Divinations: Birth, becoming, life changes, shelter, liberation, sanctuary, secrets; or blurring of consciousness, deceit, sterility, stagnation, conspiracy, insecurity

Governs:
Rebirth in the spirit
Strengthens the power of secrecy
Works of concealment and protection
To contain and hold other powers together
Realization of stillness, the Now-ness of all things
Bringing ideas to fruition in the creative process

This is the rune of maternity and represents the ready womb for child-bearing. Also represented here is the the concealment and protection of what is coming into being, in the most mundane sense, pregnancy shelters the baby until it is ready to enter this world.

Motherhood, the wisdom that comes with maturity and the patience developed by nurturing children are all mental and spiritual strengths emphasized through use of this particular rune.

Secrecy with Berkano is not a wicked thing, but a power that can be used to great effect. It is the mastery of silence as a device for listening and protecting. It is a life giving rune, so is best used to assist life, to heal and to protect. It will enhance efforts to give oneself, and others, the time and space they need to grow on their own. The creation of time and space is a magical act done consciously through restraint and silence, even concealment of one's hand in the affair altogether. This ability is magical, requires great humility and is an enviable feminine power.

C

Name: Kenaz, Kaunan, "ulcer."
Phoneme: K.
Meaning: mortality, pain.

KENAZ OR KAUNAN

Stands for:	Torch
Sound	"K"
Gods	Heimdall, Frejya
Colour	Yellow
Element	Fire
Astrology	Venus
Energy	Feminine
Health	Sexual Health, Inflammation
Key Words	Creative Energy, Lust, Knowledge, Inspiration, Clarity

RUNE KENAZ ELDER FUTHARK MEANING.

"The student surpasses the teacher."

Kenaz – Literally: "Torch" – Esoteric 'Ken' or Knowledge

Key Concepts: torch as a symbol of knowledge and intellect, illumination, searching for enlightenment, shedding light on matters, quest for truth, skills and abilities, creativity, art, craftsmanship, cunning, acquisition and application of knowledge, occult female secrets, intuition, enthusiasm in teaching/learning, study, kin-fire, opportunity, playfulness

Psi: observation, clarity of thought, cognitive faculties, humility

Energy: Controlled energy, transformation (pheonix fire), teaching/learning dynamic, illumination

Mundane: art, technique, improvement of skills, school, the stars

Divinations: Artistic or technical ability, craft, transformation, offspring, new information; or disease, decay, breakup, inability, lack of creativity, ignorance, arrogance, elitism, over-conceptualization

Governs:
Illumination (torchlight) when exploring transpersonal pathways
Creative inspiration, enthusiasm for learning
Exploration of paradigms in the search for truth
Exposing the hidden to gain new knowledge, esp. through study, reflection and new information
Strengthening of abilities in all realms
Female occult secrets
The light within, the observer

Kenaz is a remarkably powerful rune to meditate upon and contemplate, and the journey this single rune can send the seeker upon is nothing short of life long and life changing.

In the elder futhark, Kenaz means "Torch" or "Torchlight", as a source of heat and light.

Kenaz also represents the inner-fire/body heat that is passed on — as cold means death. In terms of progeny, this inner-fire is feminine: the womb, a necessary heat carried by mothers all the way back to the beginning.

D

Name: Dagaz, "day."
Phoneme: D.
Meaning: hope, happiness.

DAGAZ

Stands for:	Day
Sound	"D"
Gods	Heimdall
Colour	Yellow
Element	Fire
Astrology	Moon (waxing/waning)
Energy	Masculine
Health	Psycho-neurological problems
Key Words	Stability, Transformation, Sunrise, Polarity

RUNE DAGAZ ELDER FUTHARK MEANING.

"Time is an illusion that once realized, is lovingly embraced, none the less."

Dagaz – "Day-gahz" – Literally: "Day" or Dawn – Esoteric: Awakening

Rune of the hyper-consciousness. The process of concept becoming realized.

Psi: paradoxical truth, incommunicable experience, conceptual realization, Enlightenment, satori

Energy: twilight/dawn polarity, non-dual reality, unity, synthesis, transmutation

Mundane: another day, daylight, the inevitability of dawn

Divinations: Awakening, awareness, hope-happiness, the ideal, paradigm shift; or lack of vision, sleep, blindness, hopelessness, cataclysmic change.

Governs:
Attaining the mystical moment through penetration of the secret of paradox or non-duality
Reception of mystical inspiration – the gift of Odin.
Disappearance and the act of becoming the invisible
Invisibility as an organizing principle of Higher Consciousness
Synthesis of right-left brain dynamics.
Transformation of one thing into its opposite
Integration of female and male into complete being

Dagaz is the counterpart to time, on a daily cycle. Dagaz is a rune of bold change, for example, the burst of light at the moment of illumination. It contains within its energies the experience called 'satori', a spiritual awakening experience. It is the rune of hyper-consciousness.

The meaning of Rune Dagaz is closely connected to true desires of the heart. It is that generator of changes that come when you start working on a goal, as any growth brings transformation. Lastly, Dagaz is the Rune of polarity. It unites any polar opposites, such as life and death, darkness and light into one whole concept that goes far beyond this mundane separation based on dogma and personal experiences.

There is a legend about ancient use of Rune Dagaz that says that völvas (meaning seeress) used this Rune to become invisible by disappearing between worlds.

E

Name: Ehwaz, "horse."
Phoneme: E (long and/or short).
Meaning: trust, faith, companionship.

EHWAZ

Stands for:	Horse, or Ehwo - 2 horses
Sound	"E"
Gods	Verdandi (Norns)
Colour	Red
Element	Earth
Astrology	Gemini
Energy	Feminine & Masculine
Health	Kidneys & Liver
Key Words	Partnership, Horses, Harmony, Men, Path, Trust

RUNE EHWAZ ELDER FUTHARK MEANING.

"The mind will trust the body, the body will trust the mind."

Ehwaz – "eh-was" – Literally: "Horse" – Esoteric: Trust

Rune of harmonious teamwork and trust. Rune of pairs of entities working together for a common goal.

Psi: trust between individual entities, sexuality

Energy: trust, cooperation, the Fetch

Mundane: animals, teamwork, friendship

Divinations: Harmony, teamwork, trust, marriage, loyalty, a friend; or duplication, disharmony, mistrust, betrayal, nightmares, indecision, an enemy.

Governs:
Activating the energies of your inner Fetch
Ability to detect deceit and uncover subtle queues
Facilitates swiftness in every regard
Establishing trust and bonds with animals (ie. horse whisperers)

Ehwaz is the nineteenth Rune of Germanic Elder Futhark and the third Rune of the third Aett of Týr.

Ehwaz is a very positive Rune. It is also a very dynamic Rune.

This Rune is such a pleasant and positive Rune that even when reversed, its meaning does not pose a threat or danger.

Ehwaz symbolizes all the various bodies as vehicles for travel and movement. Ehwaz is not force, but persuasion, suggestion and co-operation.
In every way it represents flexibility, adaptability, pragmatism. It is the activation and use of instinct, using gut over the analysis or reasoning.

Rune Ehwaz point on a time when you are stepping on a path towards new beginnings and positive changes. It is the time of continuous and progressive change and development, be it person or spiritual growth.

Rune Ehwaz is effective at helping you to achieve your desired goals, to meet the right people, maintain balance and get rid of obstacles that stand on your way to success.

F

Name: Fehu, "cattle."
Phoneme: F.
Meaning: wealth.

FEHU

Stands for:	Cattle
Sound	"F"
Gods	Vanir Gods
Colour	Green
Element	Earth
Astrology	Aries
Energy	Feminine
Health	Upper Respiratory System, Joints & Bones
Key Words	Cattle, Wealth, Abundance

RUNE FEHU ELDER FUTHARK MEANING.

"Every beginning has within it the seeds of its own end."

Fehu – "Fay-Who" – Literally: "Cattle" – Esoteric: Mobile Property, New Beginnings, Wealth

Key Concepts: Wealth, money, food, sustenance, intial conditions, luck, personal power, circulation of power, financial strength, prosperity

Psi: Beginner's Mind, presence, freedom, first impressions, young love

Energy: mobility, luck, charisma, dynamic power, liquid and mobile transferable energies, abundance, circulation, 'mana', sexual attraction

Mundane: money, recent purchases, reputation, freshness, fashionability

Divinations: New beginnings, social success, foresight, energy, travel, money, control; or greed, failure, atrophy, poverty, endings.

Governs:
Delegating your energy to another, power transference or projection; the sending rune
Drawing gravity into the personal sphere
Promotion of personal and social evolution, changing circumstances of importance
Increase in personal monetary wealth
Beginner's mind and presence as a tool for consciously creating a fresh start

Fehu is actually the rune of 'luck'. Luck is a hidden but real energy field inherent in your 'hamingja'. Fehu governs the capacity to hold this luck and use it like a magical ability. This basic energy, your accumulated luck, is the foundation of the wealth and power in your life.

Fehu is associated with the life giving cosmic fire of Muspellheimr that melted the hostile ice and was thus instrumental in the creation of Midhgardhr, but will be equally so in its destruction at Ragnarok.

In starting new endeavors, Fehu will activate the will, restore self-confidence and assist in goal-setting followed by immediate action. Use the symbol and its teachings against procrastination.
Fehu is a reminder for us to act out of the present moment.

G

Name: Gebo.
Phoneme: G.
Meaning: gift.

GEBO

Stands for:	Gift
Sound	"G"
Gods	Vanir Gods
Colour	Gold
Element	Air
Astrology	Pisces
Energy	Exchanged powers, sacrifice
Health	Sexual and Mental Health
Key Words	Gift, Luck, Partnership, Connection, Generosity

RUNE GEBO ELDER FUTHARK MEANING.

"For every gift a curse."

Gebo – "Gay-boo" – Literally: "Gift" – Esoteric: Fair Exchange, Sacrifice, Sacred Marriage

Key Concepts: gifts, giving, taking, trade, sacrifice, process of exchange, balance, compensation, equilibrium, law of reciprocation, altruism, the gravity of equals and opposites, generosity, hospitality, honor

Psi: gratitude, forgiveness, appreciation

Energy: Exchanged powers, sacrifice, dissolution of barriers through gifting

Divinations: Generosity, gift, magical exchange, honor, sacrifice, divine vision; or influence buying, greed, loneliness, dependence, over-sacrifice, unbalanced behavior, dishonesty

Mundane: material gifts, thankfulness, trade

Governs:
Sex magic
Mystical union and 'Sacred Marriage' between partners
Understanding of the true meaning of gifting and binding
Giving of oneself from within
Harmony between brothers and sisters and lovers
Favours, contracts, obligations, debt and oath-taking

Gebo is perhaps one of the runes which has the most lore.

The need for exchanged energies and powers to remain equal in amounts is at the heart of the rune Gebo.

Gebo is the Rune of partnerships, friendship and things really coming together. It's the Rune of giving and receiving. The Rune calls upon joining forces with other to accomplish your goal. The Rune will help you to establish connections and strengthen the existing ones. It will help in any kinds of contracts and partnerships, establishing understanding and balance.

Gebo is also tied deeply to the exchange of sexual energies between male and female, and so it deeply governs mystical union, sacred oaths of marriage and sex magic.

Gebo is the only Rune that does not have a reversed position.

Name:Hagalaz, "hail."
Phoneme: H.
Meaning: destruction, chaos.

HAGALAZ

Stands for:	"Hail" & "Egg"
Sound	"H"
Gods	Hella
Colour	Black
Element	Water
Astrology	Aquarius
Energy	General body disharmony, hidden illnesses
Health	Sexual and Mental Health
Key Words	Hail, Union, Transformation, Protection

RUNE HAGALAZ ELDER FUTHARK MEANING.

"Don't try to fix what we should break before it breaks us."
Hagalaz – "Hag-all-az" – Literally: "Hail" or "Hailstone" – Esoteric: Crisis or Radical Change

Key Concepts: hailstones, crisis and catastrophe, disruption, radical change, destructive elements of nature, severe weather, the uncontrollable, unavoidable unpleasantness, Jungian shadow, psychoanalysis, regression, acceptance of the unalterable

Psi: disruption, change, personal past

Energy: power beyond human ability to harness, perfect pattern, seed formation, objective confrontation, destructive natural forces, chaos

Mundane: bad weather, obstacles, surprises, shelter

Divinations: Change according to ideals, changes for the long-term good, controlled crisis, corrections, completion, inner harmony; or catastrophe, crisis, stagnation, loss of power, loss of property, short-term disappointment, victim-consciousness, obsession with the past, blame.

Governs:
Completeness and balance of power, integration of unconscious shadow elements
The inevitability of Fate, Wyrd, Orlog
Evolutionary progress and operations of becoming
The outworking of a perfect pattern
Protection through banishing or exorcising disharmonious patterns, protection
Awareness of the unconscious ideas for eventual processing
Causing discomfort in others by awakening their own subconscious 'garbage'

As the ninth rune, Hagalaz has a special place in the ordering, as nine has particular significance in the elder futhark. Nine signals completion of a perfect pattern. Nine months is one of nature's most regular human cycles, that of the gestation period for a baby in a mother's womb. In this sense it is a protective rune, and assists us in acceptance of the unalterable, the seeking of shelter and patience while things blow over.

Hagalaz can be used as a curse against others, aimed to bring up their suppressed inner conflicts and thus impeding them. Hagalaz is the Rune of destruction, of a full stop and karmic debts. It is also the Rune of natural causes and disasters (hence the name Hail). For this reason the energy of the Elements has a strong influence on this Rune. It is the Rune of darkness and death. Often the events associated with this Rune are due to external influences and completely out of the control of a person.

I

Name: Isa, "ice."
Phoneme: I (long and/or short).
Meaning: cold, self-preservation, harsh reality.

ISA

Stands for:	The Ice
Sound	"I" (EE)
Gods	Verdandi (Norn)
Colour	Black
Element	Water
Astrology	Moon (Full)
Energy	Stillness, Contraction, Stasis
Health	Infertility, Anemia
Key Words	Preservation, Self-Ego, Concentration, Ice, Death

RUNE ISA ELDER FUTHARK MEANING.

"Ice only appears to stop a river's flow."

Isa – "Iss-ah" – Literally: "Ice" – Esoteric: Stasis, Stillness

Rune of concentration of things in a static or frozen state. Rune of stillness and the Ego-Self.

Psi: mental faculties, focus, ego, self-image/self-identity

Energy: stillness, contraction, stasis

Mundane: cold, self-preservation, harsh reality

Divinations: Concentrated self, ego-consciousness, self-control, unity of being; or egomania, dullness, blindness, dissipation, immobility, self-centeredness, lack of change, psychopathy.

Governs:
Development of concentration, will and focus
Halting of unwanted dynamic forces as an act of self-defense (ard against demonic influences)
Basic ego integration within a balanced multiversal system
Power of control and constraint over other wights (entities), emotional outbursts
Focus of the will into single-minded action

Isa is a rune of control. As your ego-self grows in strength through spiritual thinking and training, this construct matures into the individualized YOU (or the 'I').
Isa means Primal Matter, a stream of ice. This Rune has a connection to Niflheimr, from which the ice flows.
It's interesting to note that Isa is connected to Spring season, despite symbolizing the ice.
That said, this is not the Rune of endings. One day the ice will melt and you will break free from the stagnation moving forward with renewed energy and clear intentions.

J

Name: Jera (also Jeran, Jeraz)
Phoneme: J.
Meaning: year, good year, harvest.

JERA

Stands for:	"The Year" or "The Harvest"
Sound	"J" (PRONOUNCED Y AS IN YARN)
Gods	Freyr
Colour	Blue
Element	Earth
Astrology	Sun
Energy	Masculine
Health	Gastro-Internal System
Key Words	Time, Cycle, Reward, Fertility*, Harvest, Awakening

RUNE JERA ELDER FUTHARK MEANING.

"Patience up to a point. Know your time, but work your wyrd always."

Jera – "Yehr-ah" – Literally: "Year" – Esoteric: Harvest

Rune of harvest and reward for, or reaction to, right actions in a horizontal (naturally ordered) cyclical process. Rune of peace on the land and in the heart.

Psi: psychological time, patience, the measurement of time

Energy: good harvest, orbits, cycles, progress, biorhythms, right effort
Mundane: waiting, gardening, farming, the seasons, harvest

Divinations: Reward for positive action, plenty, peace, proper timing; or repetition, bad timing, poverty, conflict, regression.

Governs:
Fertility, creativity and harmony with the land
Peace, prosperity and plenty
Realization of the cyclical nature of the multiverse, invoking the power of time and cycles
Bringing other concepts gently into material manifestation
Initiating gradual and lasting change in flow of life

Jera is a rune of patience and movement with the harmony with natural tides of life.

Jera has to do with right timing. Jera is in the maxim "This too shall pass", the proverb, "As you sow, so shall you reap", and in the modern adage, "time heals all wounds."

Jera can magically speed things up or slow things down, and manipulation of subjective time in this manner is governed by this rune. In this rune we see the most stark western counter-point to the maxim 'time is an illusion'.

Name: Kenaz, Kaunan, "ulcer."
Phoneme: K.
Meaning: mortality, pain.

KENAZ OR KAUNAN

Stands for:	Torch
Sound	"K"
Gods	Heimdall, Frejya
Colour	Yellow
Element	Fire
Astrology	Venus
Energy	Feminine
Health	Sexual Health, Inflammation
Key Words	Creative Energy, Lust, Knowledge, Inspiration, Clarity

RUNE KENAZ ELDER FUTHARK MEANING.

"The student surpasses the teacher."

Kenaz – Literally: "Torch" – Esoteric 'Ken' or Knowledge

Key Concepts: torch as a symbol of knowledge and intellect, illumination, searching for enlightenment, shedding light on matters, quest for truth, skills and abilities, creativity, art, craftsmanship, cunning, acquisition and application of knowledge, occult female secrets, intuition, enthusiasm in teaching/learning, study, kin-fire, opportunity, playfulness

Psi: observation, clarity of thought, cognitive faculties, humility

Energy: Controlled energy, transformation (pheonix fire), teaching/learning dynamic, illumination

Mundane: art, technique, improvement of skills, school, the stars

Divinations: Artistic or technical ability, craft, transformation, offspring, new information; or disease, decay, breakup, inability, lack of creativity, ignorance, arrogance, elitism, over-conceptualization

Governs:
Illumination (torchlight) when exploring transpersonal pathways
Creative inspiration, enthusiasm for learning
Exploration of paradigms in the search for truth
Exposing the hidden to gain new knowledge, esp. through study, reflection and new information
Strengthening of abilities in all realms
Female occult secrets
The light within, the observer

Kenaz is a remarkably powerful rune to meditate upon and contemplate, and the journey this single rune can send the seeker upon is nothing short of life long and life changing.

In the elder futhark, Kenaz means "Torch" or "Torchlight", as a source of heat and light.

Kenaz also represents the inner-fire/body heat that is passed on — as cold means death. In terms of progeny, this inner-fire is feminine: the womb, a necessary heat carried by mothers all the way back to the beginning.

L

Name: Laguz.
Phoneme: L.
Meaning: formlessness, chaos, potentiality.

LAGUZ

Stands for:	Water, Sea
Sound	"L"
Gods	Nerthus & Njord
Colour	Green
Element	Water
Astrology	Waxing Moon, Mercury
Energy	Feminine
Health	Mental Health, Vascular System
Key Words	Love, Sorcery, Water, Emotion, Sea, Life Energy

RUNE LAGUZ ELDER FUTHARK MEANING.

"Our future selves call us from infinite pasts, and each night are eroded with our dreams."

Laguz – "Log-uhz" – Literally: "Water" or Ocean - Esoteric: Unconscious, Collective Memory

Rune of the unconscious context of becoming or the evolutionary process. Rune of Life's longing for itself.

Psi: emotion, psychic powers, unconscious mental processes, love, dreaming

Energy: life energy, ocean spirit, origins of life, collective unconscious, the astral plane, love as unity, evolution

Mundane: water, imagination, occultism, dreams

Divinations: Life, passing a test, sea of vitality and of the unconscious growth, memory, dreams; or fear, circular motion, avoidance, withering, depression, manipulations, emotional blackmail, lack of moral fiber, fantasy, poison, toxicity

Governs:
Transpersonal powers
Mastery of emotion in order to shape wyrd
Guidance through difficult initiatory tests, ie. initiation into life
Increase in vitality and life force
Communication between your conscious mind to another's unconscious mind
Development of 'second sight' or prophetic wisdom
All powers of dreaming (lucid dreams, astral projection)

All of life is dependent on water, and therefore Laguz represents the universal ocean, the supreme unity of all life: past, present and future.

The substance of Laguz is everywhere present, pervades all things and underlies all manifestation. It is the living energy out of which everything is made. It sustains and enriches any idea that is projected into it. The ability to see clairvoyantly and into the future are psychic talents associated with Laguz, as is protection from physical and psychic poisons.

The rune can be used in establishing a communications link from your conscious mind, under willful intent, to the unconscious mind of another.

Name: Mannaz, "man."
Phoneme: M.
Meaning: augmentation, support.

MANNAZ

Stands for:	Man
Sound	"M"
Gods	Heimdall
Colour	Blue
Element	Air
Astrology	Jupiter
Energy	Masculine
Health	Trauma, Exhaustion
Key Words	Human, Man, Collective, Internal Processes, Ego

RUNE MANNAZ ELDER FUTHARK MEANING.

"We are each a savior, each a god.
It is the fear of what this means which binds us to the realm of humankind."

Mannaz – "Man-az" – Literally: "Mankind" – Esoteric: Humankind, awareness

Rune of the Divine structure of intelligence in the human soul or psyche. Rune of the horizons of human existence and collective potential.

Psi: mind & memory (Hugin & Munin), the difference between human and all other life, development of the intellect, rational mind, perfected intelligence

Energy: psychic order of the gods reflected in humankind, projection of Self into time
Mundane: thinking, planning, analysis, the human condition, people at large (contemporary: the masses)

Divinations: Divine structure, sustainability, intelligence, awareness, social order, divine influence in life; or depression, mortality, blindness, self-delusion, collective suicide, bigotry, elitism, intellectual arrogance.

Governs:
Self-Actualization
Realization of the divine structure in humankind
Increase in intelligence, memory and mental powers (passing tests)
Unlocking the third-eye hvel, the "mind's eye"
Activating the dynamics of your own inner Christus, or Higher Self
Awareness of our roles as co-creator with the gods and nature
Mental and spiritual potential

Mannaz is the rune of human intelligence and the rational mind.
It contains information which provides answers to the deepest mysteries of Life, as well as being a storehouse of new knowledge waiting to be discovered. Mannaz is the rune of Mimir's well, for Mannaz is the rune of human consciousness which ever seeks wisdom and insight to continue its evolutionary progress toward Perfected Human.

Mannaz as a symbol can represent a number of things. Odin's two ravens, Huginn, who represents mind (thinking) and Muninn, who represents memory, is a common theme here. The symbol could also be a representation of the arch at the top of an old well, implying the power of the mind to plumb the depths of Mimir's Well: our collective unconscious or our ancestral memory.

Mannaz is our ability to analyse and predict, to wilfully generate effects and shape our individual and collective future.

Name: Naudhiz, "need."
Phoneme: N.
Meaning: need, unfulfilled desire.

NAUTHIZ

Stands for:	The Need
Sound	"N"
Gods	Skuld (Norn)
Colour	Black
Element	Water/Fire
Astrology	Capricorn
Energy	Masculine
Health	Arthritis, Joint Pain, Viral Infections
Key Words	Necessity, Distress, Loss, Karma

RUNE NAUTHIZ ELDER FUTHARK MEANING.

"Consciousness is the Necessity."
"That which does not destroy me makes me stronger." – Nietzsche

Nauthiz – "Not-this" – Literally: "Need-fire" or "Necessity" – Esoteric: Constraint, Friction

Key Concepts: Need, resistance, constraint, conflict, drama, effort, necessity, urgency, hard work, need-fire, life lessons, creative friction, distress, force of growth, the consequence of past action, short term pain for long term gain

Psi: resistance, need, effort
Energy: necessity, coming forth into being, urgency

Mundane: doing what must be done, chores, hard work

Divinations: Resistance (leading to strength), recognition of örlög (ultimate law, primal truth), innovation, need-fire (self-reliance), personal development and life lessons, achievement through effort; or constraint of freedom, distress, toil, drudgery, laxity, warnings, worry, guilt, moral cowardice, unfulfilled or unrecognized needs.

Governs:
Overcoming distress or negative örlög
Acceptance of the unchangeable
Development of magical will, the manipulation of wyrd
Understanding the dynamic force of "resistance" in the process of creating
The generation of creative energy for problem solving
Protection of one's own needs
Recognition of personal need
Love magic; especially to obtain a lover

Nauthiz (or Naudhiz) represents the need-fire, and in every way related to necessity, constraint and the inevitability of human suffering. The Nauthiz rune meaning has no reverse, but it is one of the runes whose positive and negative interpretations are closely intertwined. One doesn't really seem to come without the other. As harsh a rune as this can be, Nauthiz also reveals to us the ways of transmuting our distress into greatness and success.

Nauthiz can protect us from ourselves, but its lessons are often harsh.

Name: Othala, "inheritance."
Phoneme: O (long and/or short).
Meaning: inheritance, heritage, nobility.

OTHALA/ODAL

Stands for:	Homeland
Sound	"O"
Gods	Odin
Colour	Copper
Element	Fire
Astrology	Full Moon
Energy	Masculine
Health	Genetic Diseases, Blood
Key Words	Inheritance, Ancestral Land, Home, Property, Family

RUNE OTHALA ELDER FUTHARK MEANING.

"We inherit ourselves."

Othala – "Oh-thall-ah" – Literally: "Homeland" or "Ancestral Lot" – Esoteric: Inheritance, estate, noble

Rune of anscetral spiritual power, divine inheritance and earthly estate.

Psi: ancestral spiritual power

Energy: ancestral spiritual power, inheritance, heaven on earth, "The gift of Ing", paradise, utopia

Mundane: household, estate, inheritance

Divinations: A home or estate, group prosperity, group order, freedom, productive interaction; or lack of customary order, totalitarianism, slavery, poverty, homelessness, xenophobia, racism, genocide.

Governs:
Rightful inheritance from ancestral holdings
Collection of numinous power and knowledge from past generations
Acquisitions of wealth and property
Right understanding of global unity
Security, safety, protection, the walls of Asgard
Ascension to King amongst men
Realization of Paradise

Othala is the Rune that advises to go back to where you came from, not literally... The Rune tells you to listen to your heart and remind yourself of your ideals and morals are. It is the Rune of the ancestors and strong family ties. Your decisions and results are now based on your life experience and lessons. And yes, at times, this is the Rune of destiny in the sense that you will end up exactly where you are supposed to be. Have faith.

The ultimate realization of Othala in the rune progression is heaven-on-earth, and the homecoming of the Savior and this the final rune of the cycle. Othala means that we take responsibility for our own destinies, that the future is a continual movement toward paradise, an alignment of the inner-compass toward heaven on earth.

Othala's core power is the wise management of resources both physical and psychic. The other aspect of Othala Rune is life experience. It is everything you have learned and went through that has shaped you into a person you are today.

Name: Perthro, "source of recreation and amusement."
Phoneme: P.
Meaning: unknown. (possibly "pear-tree".)

PERTHRO

Stands for:	Dice Cup
Sound	"p"
Gods	Frigg
Colour	Silver
Element	Water
Astrology	Saturn
Energy	Feminine
Health	Renal/Urology and Female Health
Key Words	Womb, Birth, Cause & Effect, Initiation, Intuition

RUNE PERTHRO ELDER FUTHARK MEANING.

"The beginning and end are set. What's in between is yours. Nothing is in vain, all is remembered."

Perthro – "Per-throw" – Literally: unknown – Esoteric: The Norns, Fate, Lot-Cup

Rune of fate and the unmanifest. Rune of probability and the role of luck in the evolutionary process of the all things. Universe at play.

Psi: co-incidence, living with the unknown, the art and magic of guessing, pattern recognition, prophecy

Energy: evolutionary force, luck, nothingness, the unborn, the unmanifest
Mundane: gambling, random occurrences, guessing

Divinations: Good omen, knowledge of örlög, fellowship and joy, evolutionary change; or doom*, psychological or emotional addictions, stagnation, loneliness, delusion, fantasy, unknowability.

Governs:
Perception of the layers of örlög and wyrd
Manipulation of cause and effect
Placing runic forces in the stream of Nornic law
Alteration of probability and dependence on luck
The creation of favorable circumstances
Chance, gambling, divination and the art of guessing

Of all the runes, this one is the most mysterious, because Perthro deals with the mysteries within the runes themselves and the birth of the universe. Perthro is unknown is because of all the runes it represents the unknown: Fate, the unmanifest, the unknowable and the nature of chance.

Perthro represents the womb of the Goddess and something that haven't birthed yet. This is what gives this Rune the sense of magical secrecy. That secrecy, however, is now coming to light. It can symbolize hidden knowledge or even initiation.

Another ideographic representation of Perthro is a dice cup used for cleromancy (casting of lots).

Perthro is the Rune when you are ready for action. You have gone through the periods of waiting (Isa), collecting knowledge (Eihwaz) and patience. You can now move towards your goal and you will succeed.

The most important thing now is knowing your goal, having discipline and enough knowledge.

Q

Name: Kaunan, "ulcer."
Phoneme: K.
Meaning: mortality, pain.

KENAZ OR KAUNAN

Stands for:	Torch
Sound	"K"
Gods	Heimdall, Frejya
Colour	Yellow
Element	Fire
Astrology	Venus
Energy	Feminine
Health	Sexual Health, Inflammation
Key Words	Creative Energy, Lust, Knowledge, Inspiration, Clarity

RUNE KENAZ ELDER FUTHARK MEANING.

"The student surpasses the teacher."

Kenaz – Literally: "Torch" – Esoteric 'Ken' or Knowledge

Key Concepts: torch as a symbol of knowledge and intellect, illumination, searching for enlightenment, shedding light on matters, quest for truth, skills and abilities, creativity, art, craftsmanship, cunning, acquisition and application of knowledge, occult female secrets, intuition, enthusiasm in teaching/learning, study, kin-fire, opportunity, playfulness

Psi: observation, clarity of thought, cognitive faculties, humility

Energy: Controlled energy, transformation (pheonix fire), teaching/learning dynamic, illumination

Mundane: art, technique, improvement of skills, school, the stars

Divinations: Artistic or technical ability, craft, transformation, offspring, new information; or disease, decay, breakup, inability, lack of creativity, ignorance, arrogance, elitism, over-conceptualization

Governs:
Illumination (torchlight) when exploring transpersonal pathways
Creative inspiration, enthusiasm for learning
Exploration of paradigms in the search for truth
Exposing the hidden to gain new knowledge, esp. through study, reflection and new information
Strengthening of abilities in all realms
Female occult secrets
The light within, the observer

Kenaz is a remarkably powerful rune to meditate upon and contemplate, and the journey this single rune can send the seeker upon is nothing short of life long and life changing.

In the elder futhark, Kenaz means "Torch" or "Torchlight", as a source of heat and light.

Kenaz also represents the inner-fire/body heat that is passed on — as cold means death. In terms of progeny, this inner-fire is feminine: the womb, a necessary heat carried by mothers all the way back to the beginning.

Name: Raidho, "journey on horseback."
Phoneme: R.
Meaning: movement, work, growth.

RAIDHO

Stands for:	"Wagon" (ride)
Sound	"R"
Gods	Thor
Colour	Blue or Black
Element	Air
Astrology	Sagittarius
Energy	Masculine
Health	Gastro-Internal System
Key Words	Riding, Order, Ritual, Journey, Movement, Potential

RUNE RAIDHO ELDER FUTHARK MEANING.

"The journey is the destination."

Raidho – "Ride-ho" – Literally: "Ride" or "Wagon" – Esoteric: Journey

Key Concepts: the journey of Life, stories, heroism, means of transportation, right action, movement, motion, taking charge, being in control, initiative, adventure, decision-making, direction, counsel, the right path, the inner compass, leadership, kingship, nobility held by merit, moral responsibility, integrity, respect for the rights of others, innate knowledge of right and wrong, celestial procession, rituals

Psi: the story 'form' in the psyche, freedom from imprisonment, self-mastery

Energy: cosmic cyclical law, rhythm, presence (active)

Mundane: street-smarts, common sense, travel, movement, taking action

Divinations: Rationality, sound advice, action, justice, ordered growth, journey; or crisis, rigidity, stasis, injustice, irrationality, control freak, hypocrisy, wrongful imprisonment, restlessness.

Governs:
Living in the present
Access to "inner advice" and our inner compass, following the heart
Movement within one's natural limits
Blending with personal and world rhythms, consciousness of right and natural processes
Mastery of circumstance and control of situations, taking the lead
Establishment of creative rhythm in activities
Protection while traveling
Decision-making followed by immediate action

Raidho is the rune of ordered movement of energies in time and space as it pertains to human awareness. It is the rune of leading by example and of actions that speak louder than words.

Raidho is a reminder that our life is not static; it is a continuous movement, journey and transformation.

While often associated with travel and movement, Rune Raidho is much more than that. The meaning of Raidho lies in the communication area and harmonization of everything that has a dualistic nature. Raidho also symbolizes a time when you are at the end of your journey and things are finally coming together.

S

Name: Sowilo, "sun."
Phoneme: S.
Meaning: success, solace.

SOWILO

Stands for:	The Sun
Sound	"s"
Gods	Thor
Colour	White
Element	Fire
Astrology	The Sun
Energy	Masculine
Health	Skin Conditions, Burns
Key Words	Leadership, Unlimited Victory, Solar Wheel, Success

RUNE SOWILO ELDER FUTHARK MEANING.

The guide leads you to the doorway, then waits for your return."

Sowilo – "So-iölo" – Literally: "Sun" (Sol) – Esoteric: wholeness, success
Rune of guidance, goal setting and success.

Psi: central nervous system, seat of the soul, revelation, wholeness

Energy: sun-wheel, strengthening the hvel/charka, cosmic energies, motivation, life-giving force, action

Mundane: sunlight, fire, meeting of goals, confidence, taking action

Divinations: Guidance, hope, success, goals, honor, life purpose, faith in outcomes; or false goals, bad advice, false success, gullibility, loss of goals.

Governs:
Transmutation of thought into energy for action
Activating highest values
Strengthening of psychic centers (hvel aka Chakras)
Increase in spiritual will and optimal health
Guidance through the pathways, "enlightenment"
Victory and success through individual will

Rune Sowilo completes the Second Aett of the Germanic Alphabet.

It is the rune of the sun. Sowilo represents the force of fire in the physical and mental world. It promotes invigoration, dedication, optimism and persistence in any endeavor.

Sowilo is represented by the lightning. The lighting is what really ignites the Rune, giving it the power over the Fire Element.

Sowilo is a very positive Rune and yet so powerful. It is the Rune of leadership, goals and motivation that lead to success but the key here is that you have inner resources to push until you come out victorious.

Action taking is a big part of this Rune. Sowilo is the Rune of strong people. It comes with help to those who have learned how to transform their lives and their reality.

T

Name: Tiwaz, "the god Tiwaz."
Phoneme: T.
Meaning: victory, honor.

↑

TIWAZ (OR TEIWAZ)

Stands for:	The Sky Gods
Sound	"T"
Gods	Týr
Colour	Red
Element	Air
Astrology	Libra
Energy	Masculine
Health	Arthritis, Muscles, Trauma
Key Words	Justice, Victory, Law, Success, World Order, Sacrifice

RUNE TIWAZ ELDER FUTHARK MEANING.

"What is higher than the self is the Self become Higher."

Tiwaz – "Tea-waz" – Literally: "The god, Tyr" – Esoteric: Justice, Sacrifice

Rune of the balance and justice ruled from a higher rationality. The rune of sacrifice of the individual (self) for well-being of the whole (society).

Psi: spiritual warrior, honour, righteousness

Energy: sovereign order, sacrifice, right decision making

Mundane: the rule of law, fairness, peace keeping

Divinations: faith, loyalty, justice, rationality, self-sacrifice, analysis, victory, honesty, even-handedness; or mental paralysis, over analysis, over-sacrifice, injustice, imbalance, defeat, tyranny.

Governs:
Obtaining just victory and success in battle, litigation or legal matters
Building spiritual will and development of sound judgement
Develops the power of positive self-sacrifice
Develops the "force of faith" in magic and religion

Tiwaz is the Seventeenth Rune of Germanic Elder Futhark and the first Rune of the final third Aett. You will find different variations of this Rune, with the most common ones being Tiwaz, Teiwaz and Tyr.

Tiwaz is a warrior rune named after the god Tyr who is the Northern god of law and justice. Tyr is a one-handed god with a long history, and his hand was sacrificed to trick the wolf, Fenris, into being chained. Tiwaz is just victory according to the law of accumulated right past action. To rule justly, one is asked to make many self-sacrifices, and Tiwaz can develop the power of positive self-sacrifice and temper over-sacrifice.

Tiwaz is a very powerful, bright and dynamic Rune with highly strong masculine energy (the strongest in the whole Elder Futhark, as a matter of fact). The reason for that is because Tiwaz is the Rune of warriors and their spiritual guides. It is the symbol of a battleship, both spiritual and earthy.

It is an extremely fair Rune. Tiwaz represents stability, order and LAW. It is also the Rune of moral compass and internal strength to stand by what you believe in.

U

Name: Uruz, "aurochs."
Phoneme: U (long and/or short).
Meaning: strength of will.

ᚢ

URUZ

Stands for:	The aurochs
Sound	"U"
Gods	Thor
Colour	Orange
Element	Water (Ice)
Astrology	Taurus
Energy	Masculine
Health	Musculoskeletal System, Energy & Vitality
Key Words	Manifestation, Health, Wisdom, Vitality, Primal Force

RUNE URUZ ELDER FUTHARK MEANING.

"Mind over matter – matter over mind"

Uruz – "Oo – Ruse" – Literally: "Aurochs" – Esoteric: Endurance, Formation, Manifestation

Key Concepts: life force, physical health, courage, organic structure, manifestation, formation, healing, vigor, endurance

Psi: determination, persistence, freedom, courage, will, territoriality, independence

Energy: Vital formative force, archetypal patterning, raw primal power, survival, healing, endurance, manifestation, organic structuring

Mundane: physical health, stamina

Divinations: Strength, constancy, vitality, tenacity, pattern, luck, health, pragmatic knowledge, understanding; or weakness, obsession, misdirected force, inconstancy, sickness, ignorance, uncontrolled rage, insensitivity, brutality

Governs:
Shaping and forcing fortunate circumstances creatively through will and inspiration
Self-healing and maintenance of good mental and physical health
Assertion of home ground, personal space, independence and freedom
Strength and tenacity, courage, persistence against all odds
Ability to control aggression and take responsibility
Rites of passage, especially into adulthood

Uruz stands for the Wild Ox, which metaphorically symbolizes an untamed potential and drive to push forward. The Rune gives an incredible strength, dedication and power to its wearer.

The Rune of self-understanding and reflection. It is the Mother Rune of Manifestation. It can create an environment to bring fortunate circumstances and help overcome obstacles.

The Rune creates movement if the situation got stagnant and you feel stuck. It gives this fierce, aggressive and almost unconscious drive to move forward towards the unknown no matter what.

Uruz can mean personal success, often one that does not depend on a person. It is a power one cannot control. It is an unconscious drive to create and manifest. It can also indicate that you may need to act with a certain degree if aggression and persistence.

Name: Inguz.
Phoneme: Ng.
Meaning: fertilization, the beginning of something.

INGWAZ/INGUZ

Stands for:	The God Ing
Sound	"I"
Gods	Frey & Freyja
Colour	Brown
Element	Earth
Astrology	The Dark Moon
Energy	Feminine & Masculine
Health	Male Fertility
Key Words	Fertility, Energy, Children, Gestation

RUNE INGUZ ELDER FUTHARK MEANING.

"Only when we know our solitude to be different from our loneliness can we be whole enough to honor another's place."

Inguz – "Ing-guz" – Literally: "Seed" or "The god, Ing" – Esoteric: Process, space

Rune of isolation or separation in order to create a space or place where the process of transformation into higher states of being can occur. Rune of gestation and internal growth.

Psi: internal growth, personal development, the power of suggestion, the inner-child, wholeness

Energy: earth-god, stored energy, gestation process, male mysteries, subtlety, planned bursts

Mundane: male sexuality, agriculture

Divinations: Resting, gestation, internal growth, expectation, time for oneself; or impotence, scattering, movement without change, frivolity, immaturity.

Governs:
Storage and transformation of power for ritual use.
Stored Energy
Passive meditation and centering of energy and thought
Sudden release of energy
All forms of subtle, creative action

Ingwaz, Inguz or Ing is the 22nd Rune of Germanic Elder Futhark and the 6th Rune of the Aett of Týr.

Freyr was also known as Yngvi, the old Norwegian name on Ingwaz. Represented by the very ancient god image Ing, Inguz is a rune of male fertility. The English language participle "-ing" adds to any verb the idea of acton. Thus, even common elements within our most common language use "ing" to infer the process of creation.

Inguz is that potential energy that must accumulate gradually in storage before being released as a single surge of energy. Inguz governs the process of seed into catalyst, and the self-sacrifice of one form to bring into being a new form, and the characteristics inherited because of this transformation.

Inguz signals the integration of the four selves: physical, emotional, mental and spiritual. It is the drive toward completion and totality and acts as the catalyst for movement toward wholeness.

W

Name: Wunjo, "joy."
Phoneme: W.
Meaning: joy, ecstasy.

WUNJO

Stands for:	Joy
Sound	"W", "V"
Gods	Odin
Colour	Yellow
Element	Water/Ice
Astrology	Leo
Energy	Masculine
Health	Respiratory System
Key Words	Joy, Pleasure, Hope, Harmony

RUNE WUNJO ELDER FUTHARK MEANING.

"Great minds think alike, though fools seldom differ."
"Be careful what you wish for..."

Wunjo – "Won-joe" – Literally: "Joy" – Esoteric: Hope, Harmony, Perfection

Key Concepts: joy, perfection, the art of correct wishing, correct application of the will, well-being, contentment, hope, expectation, relationship, family, bonding, trusted kinsfolk, shared ideals or aims, group harmony, symbols of shared identity, optimism, cooperative effort, like-mindedness, friendship

Psi: contentment, optimism, like-mindedness, wishful thinking, shared identity

Energy: harmony of like forces, effortless ease, fellowship, fulfillment, wishing, genuine friendship,

Mundane: parties, friendship, family, community

Divinations: Joy, harmony, fellowship, accomplishment, prosperity; or stultification, sorrow, strife, alienation, warns of caution, blindness to danger, deception, betrayal.

Governs:
Strengthens links and bonds
Invocation of fellowship and harmony.
Banishes alienation and other inharmonious impediments to trust
Creating joy through the use of true will
Realization of the link and multiplicity of relationship of all things
The art of correct wishing, 'law of attraction'

Probably one of the most joyful and positive Runes of the Germanic alphabet, Wunjo brings forth the energy of pure happiness and hope, when you feel light, knowing all your troubles are now left behind. It is the Rune of pleasure, joy and everything good that is found in Odin. Other variations of his name are Wodan/Wotan/Woden and his original name depicts him as a perfect lover and peacemaker.

Wunjo is the inner urge for realization of your soul's true will to achieve perfection of consciousness and the drive to this realization in this life-time. It wards off woe and sorrow so that the abundant gifts of the multiverse have no trouble bestowing themselves upon you. In Wunjo we find harmonious energies characteristic in functional families, group affiliations, healthy societies and nations and ultimately, the world.

Name: Thurisaz, "Giant."
Phoneme: Th (both soft and hard).
Meaning: danger, suffering.

THURISAZ

Stands for:	The Giant
Sound	"TH" VOICELESS
Gods	Thor
Colour	White
Element	Fire
Astrology	Mars
Energy	Masculine
Health	Heart, Nervous System
Key Words	Destruction, Protection, Application of Power and Force

RUNE THURISAZ ELDER FUTHARK MEANING.

"If we must fight for peace then let us find our peace in battle."

Thurisaz – "Thor-is-as" – Literally: "Thurses" or "Giants" – Esoteric: Strong one, Resistance

Key Concepts: Unconscious forces, sociological forces, Thor, Loki as giant, chaos, destruction by natural forces, complexities of aggression, conflicts, disputes, psychological problems, lightning, breakthrough, aggressive male sexuality, battering down barriers, thorn of awakening, trouble, enthusiasm

Psi: enthusiasm, struggle against unconsciousness, male sexual prowess

Energy: enthusiasm, self-empowerment, chaos, active defensive force, breaker of resistance, destructive storms

Divinations: Reactive force, directed force, vital eroticism, regenerative catalyst, constructive conflict; or danger, defenselessness, compulsion, betrayal, dullness, disease, explosive violence, annoyance, strife

Governs:
Destruction of enemies, curses binds and fetters
Awakening of the will to action
Breaking resistance of blockages in body, mind and spirit
Increased potency and prowess in romantic relationships
Understanding of the division and separation of all things
Aiming the use of psychic force
The combination of right/left brain processes for generating powerful realization

Thurisaz is an old name of Thorr, it symbolizes the forces of lightning and thunder represented with Mjollnir, the hammer of Thorr. It is an extremely powerful Rune that should be used with a great deal of caution and only by one who is knowledgeable on how to control and channel Energy properly.

Why is Thurisaz so powerful and dangerous? Because it is a Rune of Cosmic Energy of Destruction and Defense (in its active form). What it means is that the Rune can be used for protection but can result in sending back the Energy with a force of a thunder, throwing back your offender.

This Rune will help to break free from limitations, to clear the path and put an order where was chaos. Thurisaz will help you to achieve this clear start but there might be a price to pay.

Name: Eihwaz, "yew."
Phoneme: I .
Meaning: strength, stability.

EIHWAZ

Stands for:	Yew Tree
Sound	"E" OR "I"
Gods	Odin
Colour	Navy Blue
Element	All
Astrology	Scorpio, Venus
Energy	Masculine & Feminine are at balance
Health	Vision, Bones, Balance
Key Words	Communication, Strength, Knowledge

RUNE EIHWAZ ELDER FUTHARK MEANING.

The path is hard and lonely and there is no end to sight."

Ihwaz (also: eihwaz) – "Yew-was" – Literally: "Yew" – Esoteric: Yggdrasil or Kundalini "The axis or process of spiritual becoming." Upper and lower worlds meeting in Midgard (earth). Rune of the mysteries of life and death.

Psi: death mysteries, the timeless, kundalini,

Energy: axis of heaven-earth-hel, secrecy, encoding, immortality, the chakra system (hvel)

Mundane: longevity, initiations, trees

Divinations: movement toward Enlightenment, endurance, initiation, protection; or confusion, destruction, dissatisfaction, weakness, death

Governs:
Initiation into the wisdom of the World Tree (Yggdrasil) and hvel (chakras)
Liberation from the fear of death.
Development of spiritual endurance and hard will to gain initiative
Spiritual vision
Communication between levels of reality – the Worlds or Yggdrasil

Rune Eihwaz is associated with a Yew tree because it represents the Norse God Odin hanging on a Tree. We all know that Odin spent 9 days on Yggdrasil Tree to learn the occult through communication with the ancestors.

The Yggdrasil or the World Tree serves as a link between the 9 Worlds and aids in astral travel, allowing the consciousness to travel between higher and lower realms.

Rune Eihwaz takes a very interesting position in the Aett. It was placed between Jera (which signifies time) and Perthro (which talks about the "open womb" that is a metaphor to things finally starting to come to birth). Eihwaz is the moment "in between" where you are rather suspended and for a reason.

Eihwaz the Rune of choice for astral travel due to its connection to the Yggdrasil Tree that serves as the link between the 9 Worlds.

_____
_____
_____
_____
_____
_____
_____
_____
_____
_____
_____
_____
_____
_____
_____
_____
_____
_____
_____
_____
_____
_____
_____
_____
_____
_____
_____
_____
_____

Z
Name: Algiz (or Elhaz).
Phoneme: Z.
Meaning: protection from enemies, defense of that which one loves.
Y

ALGIZ

Stands for:	Elk
Sound	"Z"
Gods	Valkyrjur
Colour	Gold
Element	Air
Astrology	Cancer
Energy	Feminine
Health	Immune System, Central Nervous System
Key Words	Protection, Spirit

RUNE ALGIZ ELDER FUTHARK MEANING.

"Fear has its place in every heart. Courage is only a response."

Algiz (or Elhaz) – "Al-jiz" – Literally: "Elk" – Esoteric: Protection, Higher Self

Rune of the essential link or connection with the patterns of divine or archetypal consciousness, such as the Valkyrie. Rune of the possible danger of realizing this link when unprepared.

Psi: divinity, higher self, the state of listening

Energy: protective teaching force, the divine plan, Valkyries

Mundane: protection, safety, spirituality

Divinations: Connection with the gods, awakening, higher life, protection; or hidden danger, consumption by divine forces, loss of the divine link, fear.

Governs:
Strengthening of hamingja (personal gravity, 'luck') and life force through courageous deeds
Mystical and religious communication with non-human sentient beings
Communication with other worlds, especially Asgard
Protection/defense
Receiving instruction on the magical potential of the runes
Banishing the fear of death

ALGIZ (also called Elhaz) is a powerful rune, because it represents the divine might of the universe.

Algiz is the rune of higher vibrations, the divine plan and higher spiritual awareness. The energy of Algiz is what makes something feel sacred as opposed to mundane. It represents the worlds of Asgard (gods of the Aesir), Ljusalfheim (The Light Elves) and Vanaheim (gods of the Vanir), all connecting and sharing energies with our world, Midgard.

Algiz means being a warrior and having the internal strength backed up by the powers of the Universe and Ancestors to protect yourself and others.
Rune Algiz used to be frequently seen on graveyards beside the name and dates of birth & death.

Despite the above facts, Algiz is a very positive Rune. It is not an aggressive Rune that can cause devastation or ruin. It covers a person like a cocoon, making everything negative thrown its way simply bounce back.

DATE :   /   /   ☐ MON ☐ TUE ☐ WEN ☐ THU ☐ FRI ☐ SAT ☐ SUN

The Triple Horn of Odin
This symbol contains three interlocking drink horns, they also
represent wisdom and inspiration.

THE TRIPLE HORN OF ODIN SYMBOL MEANING.

The Triple Horn of Odin can be traced back to Norse mythology, even before the Viking Age. One of the most important texts about their pagan mythology, The Prose of Edda, contains the The Mead of Poetry. Odin is the father of Norse gods and rules over all the world. He's also referred to as Wodan, Raven God, All-Father, and Father of the Slain. According to myth, Odin sought the magical mead, a mythical beverage which rendered anyone who drank it a scholar, or skald. The Triple Horn of Odin represents the vats which held the mead.

Here's how the myth goes:

According to mythology, the gods Aesir of Asgard and Vanir of Vanaheim decided to end their conflict in a peaceful way. To make the treaty official, both spat into one communal vat, which formed into a divine being named Kvasir, who became the wisest man.

Unfortunately, two dwarfs had killed him and drained his blood to create a magical mead. The dwarfs blended honey with the blood. Anyone who drank it had the gift of poetry or wisdom. They placed the magical mead in two vats (called Son and Bodn) and a kettle (named Odrerir).

Odin, the chief of the gods, was unstoppable in his pursuit of wisdom, so he searched for the mead. When he found the magical mead, he drank the whole kettle and emptied the two vats. In a form of an eagle, Odin flew off towards Asgard to escape. The myth gave rise to the popularity of mead, an alcoholic drink made of fermented honey and water, as well as the drinking horns, which were used by the Vikings for drinking and traditional toasting rituals. The Triple Horn of Odin also became strongly associated with the drinking of the mead to acquire wisdom and poetry.

A Symbol of Wisdom – Many associate the Triple Horn of Odin with the Mead of Poetry and what is obtained from it: wisdom and poetic inspiration. In the myth, whoever drinks the magic mead would be able to compose brilliant verse since poetry was associated with wisdom. Some also associate the symbol with the sacrifice needed to acquire wisdom, just as how Odin gave his time and energy for the sake of finding knowledge and understanding.

A Symbol of Ásatrú Faith – The Triple Horn of Odin has significance in Ásatrú faith, a religious movement that practices the ancient polytheistic traditions, worshipping Odin, Thor, Freya, and other gods in Norse religion.

In fact, they use a drinking horn filled with mead, wine, or beer in their rituals to honor their gods, in which the symbol emphasizes their connection with the Norse god Odin and to each other during communal gatherings.

DATE :   /   /   ☐ MON ☐ TUE ☐ WEN ☐ THU ☐ FRI ☐ SAT ☐ SUN

Gungnir, The Spear of Odin
The image of Gungnir represents power and authority.

GUNGNIR, THE SPEAR OF ODIN SYMBOL MEANING.

Gungnir, which means 'swaying' in Old Norse, belonged to Odin, and was made by the dwarves, the master craftsmen of Norse mythology. According to one story, the dwarves made the spear for Odin specially, and forged it from sunlight. According to another story, Loki procured the weapon for Odin.

In this second account, Loki cuts of the beautiful golden hair of Thor's wife Sif, and is forced to go to the realm of the dwarves to find something as beautiful to replace the hair. He approaches a group of dwarves known as the Ivaldi brothers, who agree to make a headpiece of fine gold for Sif, and enchant it to grow on her head. This second story would tie up with the idea that the spear was specifically forged for Odin from sunlight.

Of course, while in the realm of the dwarves Loki gets up to his usual mischief and he also comes home with Mjolnir for Thor and Gullinbursti for Freyr among other treasures, and ends up with his mouth sewn shut.

When Loki presents the spear to Odin he tells him that it is so well balanced that it will never miss its target, regardless of the skill of the warrior wielding it, and that oaths sworn on the spear can never be broken.

According to the Norse stories, in the early days the Aesir gods went to war with the Vanir gods, the second race of gods in the Norse pantheon. This was probably because the warlike and orderly Aesir objected to some of the more esoteric and decadent practices of the Vanir, including brother-sister marriages.

It is said that before the great battle, Odin threw his spear over the heads of the Vanir crying 'Odin Owns You All'. The two races of gods eventually made peace and hostages were exchanged. Freyr and Freya were among the Vanir gods sent to live in Asgard, and they were quickly accepted as part of the community (though their brother-sister marriage was dissolved).

Referencing this myth, it was the practice of some Viking warriors to throw their spears over the heads of their enemies before battle, and cry the same words. This was done in order to invoke the assistance of Odin in the battle to come.

As well as being the god of war, Odin was the god of wisdom, and he was known to be willing to go to great lengths in order to obtain it, even sacrificing his own eye. On another occasion, he hung himself from Yggdrasil, the tree of life, for nine days and nine nights while pierced by his own sword in order to gain knowledge of the runes. He then shared this knowledge with mankind.

In reference to this legend, whenever the Vikings sacrificed a person to Odin, they used a spear, sometimes in combination with hanging and sometimes alone.

The Vikings believed that many warriors who died bravely in battle were taken by Odin to Valhalla, in order to live until they are called on again to fight alongside the gods in the final battle of Ragnarok.

In the Ragnarok prophecy, Odin is described as leading this troupe of warriors into battle with Gungnir in hand. He then uses the spear to attack Fenrir, who kills Odin as the world ends.While this moment is not reflected in any Viking practices, it is telling that it is the moment that Gungnir, the spear of Odin, fails that the power of the Viking warriors also fails, and the world as the Vikings knew it came to an end.

DATE :   /   /   ☐ MON ☐ TUE ☐ WEN ☐ THU ☐ FRI ☐ SAT ☐ SUN

Aegishjalmur
The Helm Of Awe, it contains eight spiked tridents which
symbolizes protection and prevailing over enemies.

AEGISHJALMUR SYMBOL MEANING.

The name Aegishjalmr is a compound word comprised of two root words, 'Aegis' and 'Hjalmr'. In Old Norse, Aegis meant 'shield' and Hjalmr meant 'helm'.

The word 'helm' is itself the root word for 'helmet', a fact that becomes the source of an enormous amount of confusion over the interpretation of the word 'Aegishjalmr'. The prevalence of the word 'helmet' over 'helm' among users of the English language has fueled the misconception that the name referred to an actual, physical helmet that was worn in battle.

This rune was used to protect warriors and to instill fear in their enemies. It is comprised of eight points resembling tridents with curved prongs, all pointing outwards, and a circle in the center. It was mentioned in a collection of Old Norse poems known as the Poetic Edda, by Snorri Sturluson. In the poem, the Helm of Awe was a physical object taken from the dragon Fáfnir's hoard. Fáfnir was once a dwarf, who turned into a dragon after becoming cursed by the treasure he guarded. He used Ægishjálmr to defend his treasure against those who would try to steal it. The hero known as Sigurd slew the dragon and took Ægishjálmr from him. The symbol was utilized in later centuries and was worn between the brows of warriors to assist them in battle. It was perceived as a charm, that once drawn over the forehead would work its magic.

Aegishjalmr or the Helm of Awe was considered to be one of the most powerful and widely used Viking symbols of protection.

In Norse mythology, the symbol was believed to have been worn by the Vikings between their eyes to invoke fear on their enemies and protect the wearer against abuse of power.

In the Viking Age, warriors often inscribed the symbol between their eyebrows to show and possess strength in battle. They believed that the symbol will help them win battles, just like how it helped the dragon Fafnir.

When Fafnir spoke in the Volsungsaga, "...none dared come near me...", this was perhaps the truth of the Aegishjalmur's power to which he alluded.

Furthermore, the Helm of Awe did not only provide physical protection. It also gave the bearer mental and spiritual strength against one's own fears.

Once the bearer is able to cast away his fears, the symbol is then able to strike fear on enemies.

DATE :   /   /   ☐ MON ☐ TUE ☐ WEN ☐ THU ☐ FRI ☐ SAT ☐ SUN

Huginn & Muninn
Ravens are birds of blood and carnage, but they are also birds of wisdom and
intellect. This symbol represents both brutality and education.

HUGINN & MUNINN SYMBOL MEANING.

Huginn and Muninn are a pair of ravens who, according to Norse mythology, are enlisted in Odin's service. The birds depart every morning at dawn to fly around the Norse world, Midgard. At dinner, they return to their perches on Odin's shoulders and tell him what they have seen.

Although Huginn and Muninn might look like common ravens, they have been endowed by Odin with wonderful powers. First, the birds are able to fly the entire world of Midgard in a single day. Second, they have the ability to understand, and even speak in, the language of men. Third, they have extremely shrewd minds and wonderful powers of observation. The ravens are no mere spies for Odin; they are important advisors and confidants too.

Huginn and Muninn can also accompany Odin into battle, where they inform him of his enemy's movements and help him guide and heal his horse.

Odin's ravens' names (Huginn meaning "thought" and Muninn meaning "desire or mind") support the idea that they are projections of his consciousness. It's no great stretch of the imagination to believe that Odin, the leader of the gods, could project his "thought" and his "mind" in the same way that a shaman could and that the ravens are simply symbols of his omnipotence.

Ravens embody wisdom and guidance in Norse culture, so a god with two ravens as his flygjur would be a wise guide—just like Odin.

Huginn and Muninn frequently appear in depictions of Ragnarök, the great, apocalyptic battle where Odin is doomed to die. The ravens warn him of the event and remain on his shoulders during the battle.

Finally, some scholars believe that Huginn and Muninn are Odin's hamingja, a physical embodiment of his luck. In Norse culture, the spirit is made up of many, separable parts that can be sent on different errands. The hamingja is one of those parts, and because it is not one of the most essential parts of the spirit, it is often deployed on small missions.

It's no coincidence that Huginn and Muninn, a pair of almighty ravens, were hatched from Norse culture. Not only are ravens powerful and common symbols in Norse folklore, they played an important role in the everyday life of Norse people, too.

Mjölnir

Mjölnir is one of the most fearful and powerful weapons in existence. This symbol represents blessing, consecration, and protection.

MJÖLNIR SYMBOL MEANING.

Mjölnir is pronounced as Miol-neer. It is the name of Thor's hammer in Nordic mythology.

The name, 'Mjolnir' is commonly accepted to mean 'Lightning' in the capacity as the hammer of the God of Thunder but the root word is more similar to the words 'grind' or 'crush'. Others believe that the word may also mean 'white' and refer to the purity of white lightning.

It is widely believed that when people hear the sound of thunder, Thor and his hammer are at work.

Mjölnir is often depicted as having a large and heavy rectangular head with some intricate carvings and a short handle that only Thor can wield with one hand.

The Hammer of Thor, for all its destructive power and primary role as a weapon of war, is also a tool of rejuvenation and regeneration, and the catalyst for the rebirth of the world after Ragnarok.

The Three Versions
The first and earliest version is virtually identical to the one found in the Norse saga. The only significant difference was that Odin, the king of the Norse gods who was also known as Woden or Wotan wielded Mjolnir first, and only passed the hammer to Thor after the latter proved himself worthy.

The second version.
In it, Mjolnir is created by the Dwarf blacksmiths Brock, Etiri and Buri upon the orders of Odin. They craft it in an enchanted forge inside a dying star using a process is so powerful that it destroys the star and causes the cataclysmic events that wipe out the dinosaurs on Earth.

The third version speaks of a sentient being called the Mother Storm, a giant storm of galactic proportions that threatens Asgard. As king and defender of the realm, Odin engages it in battle, eventually defeating the mighty being and trapping it within a nugget of uru gifted to him by the Dwarven blacksmiths.

Wishing to harness its immense power as a tool and a weapon of war, Odin asked the dwarves to fashion the nugget into an object that he could wield. When the dwarves created Mjolnir upon his request, Odin found that he was unable to harness it with enough control for it to be a reliable asset.

He put the weapon aside and Mjolnir was forgotten for eons until Thor found it. He was able to lift the magical object, making it his personal weapon. This earned Mjolnir the moniker 'Hammer of Thor'.

DATE :   /   /   ☐ MON ☐ TUE ☐ WEN ☐ THU ☐ FRI ☐ SAT ☐ SUN

Svefnthorn
The Svefnthorn, which translates to 'sleep thorn', was used to put an adversary into
a deep sleep they would have trouble awakening from.

SVEFNTHORN SYMBOL MEANING.

The Svefnthorn is a popular Nordic symbol, believed to possess the power of causing someone to fall into a deep sleep. Though in folklore some people woke up from the sleep of their own accord, others could only be aroused from their slumber after the Sleep Thorn was removed. In fact, the title Svefnthorn comes from the root "svafr" or sopitor which is translated as the sleeper.

In The Saga of the Volsungs, the god Odin used a Svefnthorn to sink the valkyrie Brynhildr (Brunhild) into a slumber from which she would be unable to awaken until someone crossed the formidable circle of fire Odin had kindled around her sleeping body. The hero Sigurd was brave and capable enough to cross the flames to reach her, and so awoke her.

In The Saga of King Hrolf Kraki, Queen Olof "stuck" King Helgi with a Svefnthorn in order to knock him unconscious so that she could play a trick on him and his men. The effect wore off, apparently entirely on its own, in a matter of hours.

In Gongu-Hrolf's Saga, Vilhjalmr stuck a Svefnthorn into Hrolf's head in the night, and he didn't wake up until well into the following day when a horse rolled his sleeping body around and the thorn fell out. Here, the thorn seems to have been a physical thing of some sort that was lodged in Hrolf's head rather than "merely" a spell.

Some scholars believe that the Svefnthorn symbol is a combination of two different runes (the mystical alphabet of old Norse):

Isaz rune – This rune, also known as Isa, is a vertical line meaning Ice or Stillness. It's seen as the rune that centralises everything in an innate state.
Ingwaz rune – Getting its name from the Norse God, Ing, who was believed to be the major divine player in uniting the Jutland Vikings. It is seen as a rune of peace and harmony.
Perhaps, as the scholars suggest, the Svefnthorn, is a joining together of these two runes:

Ice \ Stillness + Peace which is quite a good description of someone who is motionless and still while in an induced slumber thanks to the Sleep Thorn.

The Svefnthorn symbol is found in a number of Norse sagas and Viking tales. Viking warriors were said to keep these symbols close by in their belief that the Svefnthorn had the power to make them feel safe from danger. This made falling asleep easy, thus allowing them to get fully rested and recharged for the next day. Some believe that it can induce sleep and help with insomnia. As such, the symbol is placed under the pillow as a remedy.

DATE :   /   /   ☐ MON   ☐ TUE   ☐ WEN   ☐ THU   ☐ FRI   ☐ SAT   ☐ SUN

The Troll Cross
The Troll Cross was meant as protection against trolls and elves. It represents
safety and deliverance from harm.

THE TROLL CROSS SYMBOL MEANING.

The trollkors (English: troll cross) is an emblem used for protection not only against trolls but elves as well—from malevolent forces, in general. A troll cross is a piece of bent iron practitioners wear as an amulet to ward off dark magic.

In the olden days, the Scandinavian people believed that iron and crosses could protect them from trolls, elves, and other dark creatures. A symbol that was spawned from this belief is the trollkors.

The Scandinavians claim that the trollkors or the troll cross has been around for a very long time, but no real archeological proof has been found.

Before the 20th century, this symbol was commonly used as a sign for home, family, and everything associated with it. It was common in their day to see the symbol around where the cows were kept because people believed it protected these animals from trolls.

The troll cross bears a striking resemblance to a Nazi symbol that was popular during World War II. This symbol's use continued after the war, by neo-Nazi groups who picked it up and many others who are not associated with the neo-Nazi.

The trollkors symbol is commonly seen on amulets. This symbol is made of a round-shaped iron with its ends crossed at the bottom possibly to mimic the shape of an Odal rune, meant to be worn as a charm since iron and crosses are believed to ward off evil entities.

The troll cross or trollkors is a metallic symbol that is believed to provide protection against negative forces. People wear it as an amulet to ward off all dark sorts of magic and evil.

In the early days, the Scandinavians used it against trolls, which are considered such big trouble in Norse mythology.

In Sweden and Norway, however, a trollkors is usually a cross-cut or carved on an object, placed above a door or window, to protect both people and property.

DATE :   /   /   ☐ MON ☐ TUE ☐ WEN ☐ THU ☐ FRI ☐ SAT ☐ SUN

Vegvisir
The Vegvisir, or That Which Shows the Way, is meant to act as a guide. It is also known as the Viking compass and a symbol for protecting one's self.

VEGVISIR SYMBOL MEANING.

The Vegvisir (pronounced VEGG-vee-seer) is an ancient Norse symbol that is believed to provide safety for those who are embarking on a long voyage. The Vegvisir is believed to have originated in Iceland.

Many Viking ships bore the Vegivisir as a talisman to protect the ship and its crew from perishing at sea.

The word "Vegvisir" is a compound of two Norse words:
Vegur which means Way, Road or Path
Visir which is translated as Pointer or Guide
The Vegvisir is known as The Pointer of the Way and was believed to help those that bore it to find their way back home when they start out on a long journey. The symbol features eight directions, symbolizing the many paths that can be taken.

The Vikings, who were great seafarers, would carry the Vegvisir with them or have it tattooed on their foreheads, as they believed it would always bring them back home.

Like anything, interpretations and beliefs are added to symbols and the Vegvisir is no exception.
Though originally believed to be an amulet that brings guidance and safety to those who are on a journey and help them find their way back home, the 20th century has seen this Norse symbol take on a more metaphysical belief. It is seen as a powerful charm for those who have no direction in life. The Vegvisir is believed to provide you with the guidance you are seeking and helps you make the right choices for your life.

It's also a reminder to the wearer that on a spiritual level, they will always be guided through the twists and turns of life and constantly find that safe harbour back to themselves as their spiritual home.

The Vegvisir is similar to the compass, in that it symbolizes safety and guidance especially during travel. Here's a quick sum up of what the Vegvisir symbolizes:

Guidance and direction on journeys
- Protection and safety
- The ability to always find one's way back home or to one's roots
- Remaining grounded and stable
- Being in control of one's own life and making the right choices on one's journey

DATE :   /   /   ☐ MON ☐ TUE ☐ WEN ☐ THU ☐ FRI ☐ SAT ☐ SUN

The Web Of Wyrd
This symbol represents the past, present, and future events in a person's life.

THE WEB OF WYRD SYMBOL MEANING.

Known as the Norse matrix of fate, the Web of Wyrd is one of the most popular and important Viking symbols. Said to have been woven by the Norns/Norni, the Shapers of Destiny, the Web of Wyrd is made up of nine staves and all the runes. This symbol is believed to interconnect and represent all the possibilities of the past, present, and future.

The word 'wyrd' comes from the Old English verb 'weorþan,' which means "to come to pass." This etymology and meaning loosely translate to how the whole concept of fate works. The word 'wyrd' is also feminine, which is said to allude to The Norns.

The 'web,' meanwhile, represents fate and how it intertwines with the past, present, and future of all beings. For the Vikings, the Web of Wyrd is a reminder that what was done in the past affects the present, and the things are done in the present will affect the future. This symbol shares the same meaning as Yggdrasil (the Tree of Life), which is known to represent interconnectedness.

Like most symbols in Norse mythology, the number 9 is a distinct feature of the Web of Wyrd. The symbol is made up of nine straight lines, said to represent its inextricable connection with the Norse mythology. Some aspects of the Norse myth that feature the number 9 are Nine Worlds, namely: Asgard, Midgard, Vanaheim, Jotunheim, Svartalfheim, Alfheim, Muspelheim, Niflheim, and Nidavellir.

Aside from the nine straight lines, the Web of Wyrd also has Rune letters in its design. These Runes are the Viking Alphabet, said to have been discovered by Odin himself. Said Runes were believed to carry the fate of the entire universe. This explains the significance of the Web of Wyrd and its connection to the destiny of all beings.

This thread is regarded as the connection between our past, present, and future, and how they are impossible to separate.

The Web of Wyrd represents fate and its complexities. This symbol depicts the connection of the fates, how our past deeds not only affect the present but the future as well.

Taken this way, the Web of Wyrd symbolizes:

Interconnection: The symbol represents the interconnectedness of all things
Destiny and Fate: As the fibers of the thread are woven together, they interconnect and become the thread of our lives.
Completion: The number 9 represents completion, and the Web of Wyrd has 9 lines.
A Network of Time: If you look at the image of the Web of Wyrd it is seen to be made up of all the runes. This reflect the idea of the intricate weaving of time, as past, present and future become interconnected.

DATE :   /   /   ☐ MON ☐ TUE ☐ WEN ☐ THU ☐ FRI ☐ SAT ☐ SUN

Valknut
It represents Odin and the power to bind and unbind and the transition from life to death and back again.

VALKNUT SYMBOL MEANING.

The name Valknut is not a traditional Viking name, but a modern Norwegian title given to the symbol. It combines the words for slain warrior, "valr", and knot "knut", to mean "knot of slain warriors". This name was chosen as the Valknut appears to be associated with the dead, and with Odin, the god of war and the dead.

Several theories have been suggested for the meaning of the Valknut. Some scholars have suggested that it was a symbol for reincarnation, others that it protected the dead soul against evil. The nine points of the triangle have been associated with the nine worlds of Norse mythology, and the three interconnected triangles have been said to reflect the connection between Earth, Heaven and Hell. The symbol has also been associated with ecstatic Seidr magic, of which Odin was a master.

Warriors who lost their lives in battle earned themselves a place in the grand hall overseen by Odin, Valhalla (Hall of the Slain) and became his adopted sons. In fact, 'valr' is the source of the English word 'valour' which we associate with great deeds of brave individuals.

Several depictions of the Valknut that have been unearthed from archaeological sites also bear the figure of Odin himself, or animals like the raven and the wolf that were his constant companions. That is the main reason why it is known as the symbol of Odin today.

The intricate design of the Valknut - which is a complex shape that can be made from a single unicursal line - renders upon it an association with mental trickery. This trickery was given a very specific name by the Norse - Seidr.

The number three has always featured prominently in both ancient and modern religions. Across millennia and across cultures spread over the world, it has been taken to represent:

The three stages of the Universe - Creation, Preservation and Destruction;
The three planes of existence - Heaven, Earth and Hell;
The Holy Trinity of Father, Son and Holy Spirit;
The three basic elements - air, water and fire;
The three periods of time - Past, Present and Future;
The three periods of life - infancy, adulthood and old age;
The concept of Body, Mind and Spirit.
The number three also features significantly in Norse mythology.

From this series of elements of the Norse sagas, we know that the number '3' was an essential part of their traditions and beliefs, both negative and positive.

The presence of three triangles in the Valknut simply gives it another perspective or another clue from which attempts have been made to decipher its meaning and use.

Yggdrasil
It is a tree that holds together the nine realms of existence with its branches and
roots. It represents life, growth, and connection between all living things.

YGGDRASIL SYMBOL MEANING.

The name Valknut is not a traditional Viking name, but a modern Norwegian title given to the symbol. It combines the words for slain warrior, "valr", and knot "knut", to mean "knot of slain warriors". This name was chosen as the Valknut appears to be associated with the dead, and with Odin, the god of war and the dead.

Several theories have been suggested for the meaning of the Valknut. Some scholars have suggested that it was a symbol for reincarnation, others that it protected the dead soul against evil. The nine points of the triangle have been associated with the nine worlds of Norse mythology, and the three interconnected triangles have been said to reflect the connection between Earth, Heaven and Hell. The symbol has also been associated with ecstatic Seidr magic, of which Odin was a master.

Warriors who lost their lives in battle earned themselves a place in the grand hall overseen by Odin, Valhalla (Hall of the Slain) and became his adopted sons. In fact, 'valr' is the source of the English word 'valour' which we associate with great deeds of brave individuals.

Several depictions of the Valknut that have been unearthed from archaeological sites also bear the figure of Odin himself, or animals like the raven and the wolf that were his constant companions. That is the main reason why it is known as the symbol of Odin today.

The intricate design of the Valknut - which is a complex shape that can be made from a single unicursal line - renders upon it an association with mental trickery. This trickery was given a very specific name by the Norse - Seidr.

The number three has always featured prominently in both ancient and modern religions. Across millennia and across cultures spread over the world, it has been taken to represent:

The three stages of the Universe - Creation, Preservation and Destruction;
The three planes of existence - Heaven, Earth and Hell;
The Holy Trinity of Father, Son and Holy Spirit;
The three basic elements - air, water and fire;
The three periods of time - Past, Present and Future;
The three periods of life - infancy, adulthood and old age;
The concept of Body, Mind and Spirit.
The number three also features significantly in Norse mythology.

From this series of elements of the Norse sagas, we know that the number '3' was an essential part of their traditions and beliefs, both negative and positive.

The presence of three triangles in the Valknut simply gives it another perspective or another clue from which attempts have been made to decipher its meaning and use.

DATE :   /   /   ☐ MON ☐ TUE ☐ WEN ☐ THU ☐ FRI ☐ SAT ☐ SUN

Sleipnir
The symbol represents eternal life, transcendence, and good luck in travel.

SLEIPNIR SYMBOL MEANING.

Sleipnir is the eight-legged horse ridden primarily by the god Odin in Norse mythology. He is the son of the god Loki (in the form of a mare) and the stallion Svadilfari who belonged to the jötunn that built the walls of Asgard.

Sleipnir is always depicted as incredibly swift and the "best of all horses", symbolized by his eight legs that carry a rider anywhere in the nine realms of Norse cosmology in record time. Since he was born of two supernatural entities, he is possessed of the power to move easily between realms, including the realm of the dead, leading to his name (pronounced Slayp-near), which means "the sliding one".

Although he is almost always ridden by Odin, in the story of the death of the god Baldr, he is ridden to the realm of Hel in the afterlife by Baldr's brother Hermóðr. Sleipnir is able to easily jump the high fence around Hel and then bring Hermóðr safely back to the gods at Asgard. The great horse also features in the tale of Odin's race with the giant Hrungnir who is killed by Thor when he threatens the Asgardians.

Sleipnir's final ride is to carry Odin to the battlefield of Vigrid at Ragnarök, the Twilight of the Gods. In the final battle between the forces of chaos that include Loki and Sleipnir's half-siblings Fenrir, Jörmungandr, and Hel – among others – on the side of chaos, most of the Norse gods are killed, including Odin and his faithful horse. Sleipnir is then thought to carry Odin to the afterlife in keeping with the traditional understanding of the horse a liminal being in Norse mythology.

Sleipnir is never depicted simply as Odin's horse but rather as his companion who shares in adventures. His death with Odin in the last great battle echoes not only their relationship but also the way a Scandinavian or Icelandic audience would have understood horses: as liminal beings able to bridge the space between the land of the living and that of the dead.

Horses were frequently included in Norse burials as they were considered essential to one's afterlife, but, as with dogs, they were also understood as guides who would bring the soul of the deceased safely to its destination.

Sleipnir falls in battle with Odin because he had to in order to ensure his friend reached the other realm safely. The horse was always understood to be in tune with the will of the gods and, through them, with the vibrations of the Universe, always knowing the swiftest way to any destination and always vigilant of their rider's safety. This idealized vision of the horse is epitomized in Sleipnir who is praised as the best of all horses not only for his speed but his devotion to the one he carries.

Triquetra
The symbols line interweaves through the circle in an unbroken flow. It is
represents unity and eternal spiritual life.

TRIQUETRA SYMBOL MEANING.

Triquetra is a Norse Viking symbol closely connected with the Valknut and Horn Triskelion.

The Triquetra or the Trinity Knot is comprised one continuous line interweaving around itself, meaning no beginning or end, or eternal spiritual life. This symbol was originally Celtic, not Norse, but with increased contact and assimilation between the Vikings and the peoples of Ireland and Scotland, the Triquetra and other Celtic symbols/motifs became culturally syncretized.

This symbol is quite ancient and has multiple meanings, which have evolved from its adoption by numerous cultures. Among the ancient Celts, anything that had three forms was considered sacred. From the three domains of existence to the three stages of life to the three elements, there was a holy meaning attached to triads. Therefore, the three sides of the trinity knot establish its versatility when it comes to interpretation. The symbol is common in a variety of faiths and cultures throughout the world.

Among the Neopagans and Wiccans, the trinity knot symbolizes the threefold character of the Goddess as crone, maiden, and mother. When viewing the Goddess as a mother, it symbolizes creation, while the Goddess as maiden represents innocence. The crone form of the Goddess symbolizes wisdom and knowledge. The symbol may also be construed to represent the forces of nature; water, fire, and earth. The three overlapping circles on the emblem represent female fertility.

It is also taken to denote the concept of time; past, present, and future, or the three forms of the universe; sky, sea, and land Some Neopagans also view it as a symbol of protection, though the basis of this interpretation is on the mistaken belief that ancient Celts attached the same meaning to the symbol.

The trinity knot can represent more than just the above meanings. Here are some other, more universal interpretations:

The knot has no beginning and no end. As such, it's the perfect representation of eternity and eternal love.
It can represent longevity and a healthy life, due to its continuous shape.
It can represent the stages of a relationship – past, present and future. Because each arc is equal in size with no single arc standing out prominently, each stage is considered equally important.

DATE :   /   /   ☐ MON ☐ TUE ☐ WEN ☐ THU ☐ FRI ☐ SAT ☐ SUN

Berserker
Symbol of bloodlust, uncontrollable rage, protection.

BERSERKER SYMBOL MEANING.

Berserker was a kind of warriors in Norse mythology. They could shift into a state of wild frenzy when becoming angry, which enabled them to engage the enemy without armor. This was also the origin of in word "Berserker" in English.

"Berserker" is composed of "Ber" and "Serk" and considered to originally mean "the warrior wearing bearskin", as it is said that they charged only wearing bearskin. Later, this word was used to refer to a fierce warrior with exceptional power. Besides, some other relevant words were also mentioned in legends, such as "Úlfhéðnar" (the warrior wearing wolf skin) and "Svinfylking" (the warrior wearing wild boar skin).

The Viking Berserkers
The so-called "Berserker" refers to a kind of tough warriors in Norse mythology. As Vikings lived in the freezing Nordic region where the strongest land animal was bear, they particularly worshipped bears. The lifestyle of Vikings determined that they were often involved in cold arms battles where physical ability was the decisive factor to the victory. Vikings worshipped bears and believed that they could obtain bear-like power when wearing bearskin. Therefore, the tall and strong soldiers in Viking troops wore bearskin, used heavy weapons such as axes, and fought as elites.

The Berserkers fought much better than common warriors, because they were physically stronger, protected by bearskin and equipped with more powerful weapons. The Berserkers always played key roles in battles, and therefore they were revered by both enemies and comrades. Belligerent Vikings left many Berserker-related legends. Belligerent Nordic warriors believed that, if they received blessings from Odin, they could acquire the "Berserker rage", the power of bear's spirit, so that they would become the Berserkers that were invincible in the battlefield.

Vikings went into battle bare to the waist and roared roughly. The extreme wrath made Vikings look usually powerful. They did not look like fighting desperately, but enjoying the pleasant sensation of desperate fights. Because they knew, the springboard under their feet was soaked by the blood of their ancestors. And their descendents would continue the desperate fights on the same springboard. They could not fail either their ancestors or their descendants.

Every Viking was proud of being a Berserker and killing enemy Berserkers. Nobody knows why such primitive type of battles stimulated so amazing human nature, but the stories of Berserkers will be passed down from generation to generation as part of the spirit of Vikings.

Axe

The axe symbol stands for strength and bravery, the ability of one's heart or mind to cut through any obstacles on their life path.

AXE SYMBOL MEANING.

As a symbol, the axe stands for bravery, strength, and audacity. It is a reminder of heritage and the accomplishments of ancestors who bent the world to their will using only what they had. It is a symbol of the berserker, and all that entails. It conveys the heart or mind's ability to cut through that which holds one back and to forge boldly ahead.

The Axe that was used by warriors then was shaped differently from the axes in use today. The Viking Axe came in different sizes, from the small hand axes to the larger battle-axes with thinner blades that are often seen in illustrations and films depicting Viking warriors.

A distinct feature of the Viking Axe is that it is in a single bit form, which makes it easier to use during battles. The axe was a handy tool for Vikings that did not require as much time to make. Yet it is one of the sturdiest and most useful weapons of the warriors in battle.

It is said that every Viking owned an axe since childhood because apart from being a weapon the axe was also used in farms and homesteads. Everyone during the Viking Age had an axe that was used for various purposes—from intimidating invaders to chopping wood.

The axe has always been a formidable symbol of strength and bravery. From the 9th century up to the modern times, the Viking Axe was either carried, kept or worn as a pendant, a symbol that meant victory in all pursuits.

In Norse mythology, military apparels always featured an axe because it signifies bravery and power. For the Vikings, the axe was a tool, a weapon and protection from evil spirits.

Every Viking carried with him similar protection from evil spirits, which also helped him win in battle and return to his tribe with his shield and not on it.

The Viking Axe in any form is believed to be available only to the brave and strong, who are always prepared to face all obstacles that arise in their path.

DATE : / / ☐ MON ☐ TUE ☐ WEN ☐ THU ☐ FRI ☐ SAT ☐ SUN

Gullinbursti
The boar symbol meant happiness, peace, and plenty for the Vikings.

GULLINBURSTI SYMBOL MEANING.

Among the animal world in Norse mythology, Gullinbursti must be quite an obscure name. Many hear about Sleipnir Odin's horse that no one could ever outrun him. But Gullinbursti was quite unpopular. This blog post is to tell some stories about Gullinbursti the Boar

Gullinbursti was the golden boar of Freyr the God of Summer and Storm. Freyr was the son of Njord Aesir Chief God coming to live in Asgard. Legend had it that the Vikings worshipped Njord for his power of fertility and summer. Because only in the summer could the Vikings grow their food for the years. When winter was coming, it was so harsh to live, not to mention going out and cultivating.

Gullinbursti was made from the most talented craftsmen in the Nine Cosmos – the dwarf. When Loki came to Svartalfheim to ask the dwarves to create some treasure for the gods, Gullinbursti was one of the treasure.

It seems that Freyr and his golden boar Gullinbursti were closely linked, and Gullinbursti was the primary attribute of the god. While Gullinbursti was regularly used to represent the god, the same is not true of his other treasures, the ship Skidbladnir, and a magical sword that had the power to fight on it own.

Warriors would often place images of Gullinbursti on their helmets and shields. Gullinbursti was probably more a symbol of luck than protection. Freyr was a god of abundance, and may have been called on to reward warriors with copious booty. Gullinbursti may also have been a symbol of courage, as boars are notoriously fierce.

Gullinbursti, which means Golden Mane or Golden Bristles in Old Norse, was said to shine so brightly that it could illuminate even the darkest night. Gullinbursti could also run through the air and over water, and was better than any horse.

Freyr the god rode on the Gullinbursti the Boar to enter Ragnarok. Scholars believed that Gullinbursti also fell in this final battle with Freyr. In the last battle of Ragnarok, Freyr encountered Surtr the giant of fire. The two had an intensive combat which finally led to the death of Freyr.

Either way, Gullinbursti was an appropriate symbol for Freyr as one of the Vanir gods, as the Vanir were considered more wild and unpredictable than the Aesir, and boars were famously unpredictable.

His sister Freya was also associated with the animal, and was accompanied by her own boar Hildisvini. The golden color of Gullinbursti was no doubt a reference to Freyr's role as a god of sunshine, wealth and abundance.

Back to the Viking Age, animals like goat or boar were common for the Viking community. From these kinds of animals, the Vikings could have not just food but also skin, bones, and milk.

DATE :   /   /   ☐ MON ☐ TUE ☐ WEN ☐ THU ☐ FRI ☐ SAT ☐ SUN

FREYA
As a goddess of love, sexual lust, and fertility, Freya has a symbolic meaning
similar to that of goddesses such as Aphrodite and Venus.

FREYA SYMBOL MEANING.

Freya, also spelled Freyja, is a Nordic goddess of fertility, beauty, love, sex, as well as war and seiðr - a special kind of Norse magic. A beautiful and powerful goddess, Freya sits at the top of the pantheon of Norse Vanir deities, opposing the other faction of Norse gods - the Æsir or Asgardians.

The name Freya in Old Norse translates to Lady. The name is said to have been derived from the Proto-Germanic word 'frawjon' which was the title used for a mature woman with an upper-class social status. The name is also believed to be the root of the modern German word 'frau' which is the title given to a married woman. Some also believe that Friday could have been derived from Freya, since the day is said to be Freya's day. And because her lucky number was 13, Friday 13th is said to be her feast day, when she is celebrated.

The most common symbol associated with Freya is the Brisingamen Necklace - a necklace that sparkled and shined so beautiful that Freya was willing to go to extreme lengths to have it.

Legend states that one night, Freya wandered into the land of the Dwarfs. There, she saw four of them making the most beautiful golden necklace. She told them that she would pay them any amount of gold and silver for it.

However, the Dwarfs were not interested in money. They told Freya that the only way they would give her the Brisingamen was if she would sleep with each one of them. Freya loathed the idea of sleeping with the hideous Dwarfs, but her desire burned so strongly for the Brisingamen that she agreed to their demands. After four nights of sleeping with each one, they made good on their deal, and gave it to her. Another symbol Freya is associated with is her golden chariot pulled by two blue cats, a gift from Thor. Sometimes she also rode the boar Hildisvini, who was her faithful companion.

Freya also the mother goddess in the Vanir pantheon, a defender war goddess to her people, and a ruler of the realm to which fallen heroes go to await Ragnarok.

Even just as a goddess of love, Freya is very different from most of her counterparts from other cultures. Where most goddesses of love and sexual lust are portrayed as seductresses and the initiators of love affairs and sexual acts, Freya is portrayed as a mourning goddess who is desired by all but is trying to be faithful to her missing husband.

Being one of the Vanir leaders, Freya is considered very powerful. Some might say she is the most powerful Vanir goddess to have existed. Freya remains an influential goddess, and plays a central role in Norse mythology.

DATE :   /   /   ☐ MON ☐ TUE ☐ WEN ☐ THU ☐ FRI ☐ SAT ☐ SUN

FREYR
The Norse god of peace, virility, fertility, prosperity and sacral kingship. He's also associated with good weather, sunshine and a bountiful harvest.

FREYR SYMBOL MEANING.

Freyr is one of the main Vanir gods in Norse mythology but he was also accepted as an honorary Æsir (Asgardian) god in Asgard after the Æsir-Vanir War. A twin brother of Freya and a son of the sea god Njord.

Freyr is described as the Norse god of fertility, peace, prosperity, sascral kingship, and virility. Additionally, he is associated with good harvest, good weather, and sunshine. While he is often portrayed as a handsome man wearing simplistic or farming clothes, he is also depicted as a god of glamor. He is accompanied by a magical golden-bristled boar which is known as Gullinbursti and he carries a powerful sword that can fight his enemies on its own.

Freyr is considered a member of the Aesir gods because he became a resident of Asgard after the Aesirr-Vanir war. He was Njord's (the god of the sea) and Nerthus' (Njord's sister) son. Additionally, he was Freya's twin brother and her husband when they were still at Vanaheim. Freyr kept sacred horses at his sanctuary in Trondheim, and he had invested all his time and resources in the horse cult.

Freyr was also known as Yngvi. Norse mythology describes Yngvi as the forefather of the Yngling lineage, which was one of the legendary dynasties of Swedish kings. It is from the Yngling lineage that the earliest Norwegian kings descended. Additionally, 'Yngvi' is the true name of the Norse god Freyr, who was associated with fertility, sunshine, and rain.

Freyr is often depicted with his boar by his side hence the boar is considered his sacred animal. The boar is associated with both war and fertility. Freyr's golden boar "Gullinbursti" had a bristle that shone brightly in the middle of the night and guided Freyr whenever it was dark. Also, Freyr is associated with symbols such as pigs, which are closely related to the boar.

Also, he is associated with symbols such as farms, fields, harvest symbols, crops, pollen, seeds and unprocessed foods. The Norse people believed that they would receive abundance during harvest if they invoked the name of god Freryr.

Another symbol of Freyr is the sword , antler or horn. Most Icelandic sources claim that Freyr fights at the Ragnarok using the horn of an elk, which seemed a better alternative to a sword. Additionally, he often yields up his mighty sword during special events.

He is also associated with virile male animals, such as stallions, bulls, and stags, which directly represent his masculine nature. His presence was welcomes with merry so he is associated with festivals, feasts, and bawdy humor.

Another symbol of the fertility god, Freyr, is the phallus. He is portrayed with a large, erect phallus, which is often a representation of his sexual virility and fertility.

DATE :   /   /   ☐ MON ☐ TUE ☐ WEN ☐ THU ☐ FRI ☐ SAT ☐ SUN

Fenrir
The Symbol represents loyalty, strong family ties, good communication, education,
strength, ferocity, destiny, and inevitability.

FENRIR SYMBOL MEANING.

In Norse mythology, Fenrir is the son of the god Loki and the giantess Angrboða. His siblings are the world serpent, Jörmungandr, and the goddess Hel. All three of them were prophecized to help bring the end of the world, Ragnarok. While Jörmungandr's role was to start Ragnarok and then battle Thor, Fenrir was the one who would kill the All-Father god, Odin.

The name Fenrir comes from Old Norse, meaning a fen-dweller. Fenrisúlfr was also used as it meant Fenrir's wolf or Fenris-wolf. Other names for the monster were Hróðvitnir or fame-wolf, and Vánagandr which meant monster of the [River] Ván. In all legends, Fenrir was prophecized to kill Odin during Ragnarok and then be killed himself by Odin's son Víðarr. Because the gods themselves also new the myth of Ragnarok, they new Fenrir's role in it from before the wolf was born. So, when Fenrir, Jörmungandr, and Hel were born, the gods took steps to avoid their role in Ragnarok.

Jörmungandr was tossed in the great ocean that encircled Midgard
Hel was brought to Niflheim where she would be the goddess of the Underworld
Surprisingly, Fenrir was raised by the gods themselves. He was kept away from Loki, however, and was instead entrusted to the god Týr – son of Odin and the god of law and war, Týr was similar to the ancient Greek god, Ares.
Týr was supposed to "keep Fenrir in check" and the two became good friends. Once the wolf started getting dangerously large, however, Odin decided that more drastic measures would be needed and Fenrir would have to be chained.
To chain the giant wolf the gods tried three different bindings.
First, they brought the binding called Leyding and lied to Fenrir that they just want to test if he was strong enough to break it. The wolf broke Leyding with no effort, so a second binding was devised.

Dromi was a much stronger binding and the gods promised Fenrir great fame and fortune if he could break through it. This time the wolf struggled a little, but broke Dromi as well. Truly scared this time, the gods decided that they'd need a special type of binding for the giant monster.
Gleipnir was the third binding and it was peculiar, to say the least. It was crafted from the following "ingredients":
The roots of a mountain
The spittle of a bird
The beard of a woman
The sound of a cat's footfall
The sinews of a bear

Wolves were seen as both being negative and positive to the Norse people. On one hand, they can represent chaos and destruction (e.g. Fenrir, Skoll, and Hati), while on the other hand, they can also represent bravery, loyalty, protection, and wisdom. Fenrir was often viewed as someone wrongfully chained in an attempt to prevent the fulfillment of his destiny.

DATE :   /   /   ☐ MON ☐ TUE ☐ WEN ☐ THU ☐ FRI ☐ SAT ☐ SUN

Jörmungandr
The symbol for the eternal cycle of life, death, and rebirth.

JÖRMUNGANDR SYMBOL MEANING.

Jormungandr (pronounced "YOUR-mun-gand) is a sea serpent based in Norse mythology. The name itself means "huge monster." Ironically, when Jörmungandr was born, Odin tossed the then-still-small serpent into the sea out of fear. And it was exactly in the sea that Jörmungandr grew undisturbed until it earned the moniker World Serpent and fulfilled his destiny.

Jormungandr was brother to two further children of the giant couple, the giant wolf Fenrir, and the giantess Hel. Of the three of them, Jörmungandr's forewarned destiny was definitey the most significant - the giant serpent was prophesied to grow so large that he'd encompass the whole world and bite his own tail. Once Jörmungandr released his tail, however, that'd be the beginning of Ragnarok - the Nordic mythological cataclysmic "End of days" event.

By far the most important role that Jormungandr has to play in Norse mythology is as part of Ragnarok, the prophesized battle at the end of the world in which the Aesir gods and giants will fight to the death, and cause the total destruction of the Norse cosmos.

It may be that Jormungandr himself triggers Ragnarok. According to Norse mythology, the apocalypse will be preceded by three years of relentless winter in Midgard, the world of men.

Jormungandr will become uncomfortable in the icy waters that surround Midgard, and make his way to the surface. His huge bulk means that this movement will cause powerful earthquakes across the nine worlds of the Norse Cosmos.

These earthquakes will allow his brother, the wolf Fenrir, to break the chains that hold him in Asgard. It will also allow his father Loki to escape his prison.

He has been chained to two rocks, with a venomous serpent dripping painful venom onto his skin, for his role in the death of Balder, a son of Odin and the most beloved of the Aesir gods.

Loki will lead an army into Asgard to fight the Aesir gods, and will fight to the death with the Aesir god Heimdall. Fenrir will devour Odin himself, before being slain by one of Odin's sons.

In the final battle Jormungandr will find himself facing Thor one final time. Thor will fight harder than he has ever fought before and eventually pummel the Midgard Serpent to death with his hammer.

However, after his victory, Thor will be covered in so much of Jormungandr's venom that he will only be able to walk nine steps before falling to his own death.

Jormungandr will breathe so much of his poison into the air that he will poison all of the nine worlds of the Norse cosmos.

Jörmungandr is a pivotal figure in Norse mythology, and remains an awe-inspiring, frightening figure. He signifies the inevitability of destiny and the one that brings about the battle that ends the world.

DATE :   /   /   ☐ MON ☐ TUE ☐ WEN ☐ THU ☐ FRI ☐ SAT ☐ SUN

Hel
The Norse goddess of the dead and queen of the underworld. She is seen as a goddess of ancestral wisdom.

HEL SYMBOL MEANING.

Hel (meaning Hidden) is the daughter of the god of mischief Loki and the giantess Angrboda. Hel also has two brothers from the same union – the giant wolf and slayer of Odin Fenrir and the world serpent and killer of Thor, Jörmungandr.

Odin sent her to Niflheim, one of the Norse lands of the dead, and gave her jurisdiction over the realm. This was the place where the Norse dead that did not die on the battlefield found themselves. Warriors that died in battle were taken either to Valhalla, the hall of Odin, or Folkvangr, the hall of Frigg. This underworld is also often called Helheim but that name seems to have appeared in later authors only to help distinguish the person from the place. Hel, the place, was said to be located in Niflheim – an ice-cold realm which translates as World of Mist or Home of Mist. As the goddess of the underworld, she had responsibility for hosting the souls that found themselves there.

Earlier sources describe Helheim as located beneath one of the three roots of Yggdrasil, the world tree, with the other two roots leading to Jotunheim, the realm of the giants, and Midgard, the world of men.

The goddess of the underworld guarded the realm of the dead, and the goddess of death is described in some stories as appearing to those destined to die, telling them that they would soon join her in her realm.

In all the stories from Norse mythology, the goddess of death plays her most important role in the death of Balder.

When Balder, beloved son of Odin and Frigg, is slain in a game, thanks to the machinations of Loki, Balder finds himself in Helheim.

Devastated by the loss, Odin and Frigg send Hermod, another of the Aesir gods, to Helheim in order to ask Hel, as goddess of the underworld, to allow Balder to return to the world of the living.

Hermod pleads with Hel, explaining that Balder is the most beloved being in the Norse cosmos, and therefore should be returned.

The goddess of death actually agrees to return Balder, but only on the condition that every single thing in the Norse cosmos weeps for him, as proof of this universal love. The Aesir gods successfully ask all things to weep for Balder. Only one giantess, thought to be Loki in disguise, refuses to weep. Therefore, the goddess of death kept her prize.

Balder stayed in Helheim as a companion of Hel until Ragnarök, when the chaos that spread across all the worlds of Norse mythology allowed him to return to Asgard and fight alongside the other Aesir gods.

Hel is a cold, uncaring character in Norse mythology who was neither good nor evil. As the ruler of one of the places where the Norse were believed to go after death, she had an important role. However, she doesn't feature prominently in many myths.

DATE :   /   /   ☐ MON ☐ TUE ☐ WEN ☐ THU ☐ FRI ☐ SAT ☐ SUN

Loki
Kenaz is considered Loki's rune, because it's a rune that is strongly represents
knowledge and power.

LOKI SYMBOL MEANING.

Loki was the son of the giant Farbauti (meaning Cruel Striker) and the giantess Laufey or Nál (Needle), depending on the myth. Whether god or giant, Loki was first and foremost a trickster. Many Norse myths include Loki in one way or another, usually as a chaotic force that runs amok and causes unnecessary, and often fatal, problems. There are occasional "good deeds" that can be attributed to Loki as well but more often than not their "goodness" is a byproduct of Loki's mischievousness and not its intent.

In Old Norse the word 'loki' means knot or tangle, and he may have been considered responsible for some of the misfortunes that befell men, and therefore be a kind of trickster god, but there is little evidence for this. Loki's most prominent symbol was the snake. He's often depicted together with two intertwined serpents. He's also often associated with mistletoe, for his hand in Baldur's death, and with a helmet with two horns.

Loki has been described in many Poetic Edda poems as the "blood brother" of Odin, or in some cases, the brother of Thor. For this reason, he is often associated with the Aesir gods - a group of warrior and ruler gods who at one point in time fought against the Vanirs (deities of agriculture, fertility and commerce).

Loki's origin actually traces to the Jötunns - a race of giants and malicious mythical beings that were often the sworn enemies of the Aesirs and the Vanirs.

There are very few artistic depictions of Loki from the ancient Norse, one of which is the Snaptun Stone, which features a man with his lips stitched together. There is also a myth that tells of Loki getting his mouth sewn shut by dwarves.

Loki's appearance receives more attention when he is shapeshifting.
In his misadventures causing chaos and mayhem, he takes the form of an old woman, a giantess, a flea, an eagle, a mare, a seal, and a salmon, among others. There may be more Norse artistic depictions of Loki in existence, but they are of him in an alternate form.

Besides snakes, Loki is often associated with nets.
Loki creates real and metaphorical nets. He crafts nets to catch salmon, and entraps gods and mortals into his schemes.
But Loki is often caught in his own nets, sometimes literally. In the same myth that depicts Loki inventing the perfect fishing net, he turns himself into a salmon, only to be caught in that net by Thor. When the gods chain Loki to a rock, he is bound by his own son's intestines-ropes that Loki indirectly created.
Because Loki tends to be caught in traps of his own design, Jormungandr makes a fitting symbol for him, a snake eating his tail.

Loki's symbol, if he has one, is not known. Even today, Loki remains elusive, changeable, and unknowable.

DATE :　　/　　/　　☐ MON ☐ TUE ☐ WEN ☐ THU ☐ FRI ☐ SAT ☐ SUN

Viking Rune
Symbol of protection

DATE :   /   /   ☐ MON ☐ TUE ☐ WEN ☐ THU ☐ FRI ☐ SAT ☐ SUN

Viking Rune Gibu Auja
Good Luck

Viking Rune
Health

DATE :   /   /   ☐ MON ☐ TUE ☐ WEN ☐ THU ☐ FRI ☐ SAT ☐ SUN

Viking Rune
Protection and Accumulation of one's Force

DATE :   /   /   ☐ MON ☐ TUE ☐ WEN ☐ THU ☐ FRI ☐ SAT ☐ SUN

Viking Rune
Health, Long Life

DATE :   /   /   ☐ MON ☐ TUE ☐ WEN ☐ THU ☐ FRI ☐ SAT ☐ SUN

Viking Rune
Strength

DATE :   /   /   ☐ MON ☐ TUE ☐ WEN ☐ THU ☐ FRI ☐ SAT ☐ SUN

Viking Rune
Eternal Love

DATE :   /   /   ☐ MON ☐ TUE ☐ WEN ☐ THU ☐ FRI ☐ SAT ☐ SUN

Viking Rune
Determination

DATE :   /   /   ☐ MON ☐ TUE ☐ WEN ☐ THU ☐ FRI ☐ SAT ☐ SUN

Viking Rune
Endurance

DATE :   /   /   ☐ MON ☐ TUE ☐ WEN ☐ THU ☐ FRI ☐ SAT ☐ SUN

Viking Rune
Spiritual and mental power

DATE : / / ☐ MON ☐ TUE ☐ WEN ☐ THU ☐ FRI ☐ SAT ☐ SUN

Viking Rune
Wisdom

DATE :   /   /   ☐ MON ☐ TUE ☐ WEN ☐ THU ☐ FRI ☐ SAT ☐ SUN

Viking Rune
Safe Travels

DATE :   /   /   ☐ MON   ☐ TUE   ☐ WEN   ☐ THU   ☐ FRI   ☐ SAT   ☐ SUN

Viking Rune
Courage

DATE :   /   /   ☐ MON ☐ TUE ☐ WEN ☐ THU ☐ FRI ☐ SAT ☐ SUN

Viking Rune
Peace

DATE :   /   /   ☐ MON ☐ TUE ☐ WEN ☐ THU ☐ FRI ☐ SAT ☐ SUN

Viking Rune
Victory

DATE :   /   /   ☐ MON ☐ TUE ☐ WEN ☐ THU ☐ FRI ☐ SAT ☐ SUN

Viking Rune
Love

Viking Rune
Hope

DATE :   /   /   ☐ MON ☐ TUE ☐ WEN ☐ THU ☐ FRI ☐ SAT ☐ SUN

Viking Rune
Inspiration

Viking Rune
Success

Printed in Great Britain
by Amazon

15060907R00072